SOCIAL PROTECTION SECTOR STRATEGY

FROM SAFETY NET TO SPRINGBOARD

The World Bank
Washington, D.C.

Library of Congress Cataloging-in-Publication Data
Social protection sector strategy: from saftey net to springboard.
    p. cm.
  Includes bibliographical references.
  ISBN 0-8213-4903-1
  1. Social security—Developing countries. I. World Bank.

HD7252 .S62 2001
362'.00425'091724—dc21   00-066780

CONTENTS

As the World Bank moves toward a broader understanding of poverty reduction and the relationship of risk to poverty, the standard concepts and interventions of social protection are no longer sufficient. This first sector strategy paper for social protection reflects this view and argues for the development of social protection programs that not only help poor women and men cope with the result of downturns (a safety net), but proactively help them take on higher return activities with less concern about the risks (a springboard). Such an approach provides the opportunity for people to move out of poverty while still providing support for those in most severe need.

Implementation of this sector strategy paper's conclusions would help move the World Bank's analytical and lending work toward a more holistic, client-driven agenda. Specifically, the strategic directions would expand the World Bank's support for informal and market-based social protection arrangements, resulting in, for example, more community-driven development interventions and an increased role for the private sector in skills building. The strategy would involve refocusing support for public sector social protection programs toward (a) traditionally underserved groups (for example, by moving from reforming formal pension systems to looking more broadly at old-age income security for the lifetime poor) and (b) a more comprehensive reform agenda (for example, by addressing safety net reform more clearly within the context of changing labor market circum-

stances) and (c) more support for risk reduction and mitigation (for example, by providing school vouchers instead of cash handouts). The strategy paper also outlines areas in which its conceptual framework, social risk management, may be useful to other sectors and thematic areas of work. The World Bank's regions have already applied it successfully in the development of regional and country-specific action plans.

With the adoption of the strategy, the World Bank stands ready to renew and focus the policy dialogue with client countries around social protection issues and to offer support to governments in implementing specific social protection instruments. The implementation of this strategy will strengthen our role as a credible partner in the fight against vulnerability and poverty.

v

Eduardo Doryan
Vice President and Head of Network,
Human Development Network

Robert Holzmann
Director,
Social Protection

Steen Lau Jorgensen
Sector Manager,
Social Protection

Arvil van Adams
Sector Manager,
Human Development, Sub-Saharan Africa

Alan Ruby
Sector Director,
Human Development, East Asia and the Pacific

Michal Rutkowski
Sector Manager,
Social Protection, Europe and Central Asia

Ana-Maria Arriagada
Sector Manager,
Social Protection, Latin America and the Caribbean

Zafiris Tzannatos
Sector Manager,
Social Protection, Middle East and North Africa

Roberto Zagha
Sector Director,
Poverty Reduction and
Economic Management, South Asia

ACKNOWLEDGMENTS

A team of technical specialists from the social protection sector of the Human Development Network of the World Bank prepared this Sector Strategy under the guidance of the Social Protection Sector Board. The process also involved staff and managers in other sectors of the World Bank Group.

Robert Holzmann (Director, Social Protection) and Steen Jørgensen (former Sector Manager, Social Protection and current Director, Social Development) led the work. Christine Allison, Amit Dar, Margaret Grosh, Ian W. Mac Arthur, Anita Schwarz, Lynne Sherburne-Benz, and Paul Siegel, among others, were major contributors. The report benefited from consultation with other members of the World Bank Group, a number of external agencies, and an External Advisory Panel consisting of Tarsicio Castaneda, Nieves Confesor, Frank Field, Peter Heller, Michael Lipton, July Moyo, Rani Parker, and Igor Tomes.

The paper drew on strategies elaborated by teams responsible for social protection in each of the World Bank's six regions. Jill Armstrong (East Asia and the Pacific), Ana-Maria Arriagada (Latin America and the Caribbean), Trina Haque (Sub-Saharan Africa), Mansoora Rashid and Michal Rutkowski (Eastern Europe and Central Asia), Zafiris Tzannatos and Setarah Razmara (Middle East and North Africa), and Tara Vishwanath (South Asia) headed up these efforts. Manny Jimenez, formerly of the Development Economics Group, and Michelle Riboud, of the World Bank Institute, made contributions regarding the activities of their respective units on social protection issues.

This is the first World Bank Strategy Paper for the social protection sector, one of the World Bank's youngest sectors. The preparation of this paper has offered the opportunity to rethink the concept of social protection, take stock of the World Bank's experience in this area, and develop the strategic thrust of future work. This paper highlights the need to expand the definition of social protection to encompass all public interventions that help individuals, households, and communities to manage risk or that provide support to the critically poor. It also recommends that social protection programs be embedded in an integrated approach to poverty reduction based on a new framework for social risk management.

BACKGROUND

The World Bank's involvement in social protection—which traditionally consists of labor markets, pensions, social funds, and "safety nets"—began with work on labor markets in the 1970s and the incorporation of safety net components into structural adjustment programs in the 1980s. The debt and economic crises of the 1980s in various parts of the world set the stage for the *World Development Report 1990* on poverty, which recognized the importance of safety nets. The concept of social protection gained importance with the collapse of communism, the continuation of economic crises, and the rising share of elderly populations in developing countries. The World Bank espoused a broader view of social protection in its *World Development Report 1995*, which focused on labor issues, as well as in its groundbreaking 1994 study of aging and pension reform, *Averting the Old Age Crisis*.

Events of the 1990s brought social protection programs to the forefront of the World Bank's work. The fiscal impact of the "cradle-to-grave" social security schemes in the former communist countries was unsustainable, and the World Bank's approach entailed reducing expenditure and targeting transfers to cushion the negative effects of transition on the most vulnerable. The global financial crisis that hit East Asia and then Russia and Brazil in 1997-98 resulted in the implementation of large-scale social protection measures with World Bank assistance. The crises and the downturn in the East Asian "miracle" countries demonstrated that growth and sound macroeconomic policies, while necessary, are insufficient for sustained poverty reduction. Shock-resistant risk management programs, including safety nets, income support systems for the elderly, and well-functioning labor markets with social safeguards are essential to reduce poverty over the long term and to protect gains already made.

The World Bank's portfolio in social protection reflects its growing involvement in the sector in response to world conditions. Lending in the social protection area has increased more than six-fold since 1994. The lending volume in FY99 was $3.76 billion, 13 percent of the World Bank total (all monetary figures are in US dollars). While the response to the global financial crisis has driven much of the recent increase, annual lending levels for investment operations and noncrisis reform are about $3/4$ of a billion and 1 billion dollars, respectively.

In FY99, the social protection portfolio consisted of 92 purely social protection loans, with a commitment of $6 billion. Another 183 loans contained significant social protection components, adding $8.9 billion (making an overall portfolio of $14.9 billion). The limited evidence that exists on the quality and effectiveness of the portfolio is generally positive, as measured by the World Bank's Operations Evaluations Department and Quality Assurance Group, although there are emerging signs of strain regarding the quality of portfolio supervision.

The World Bank's experience with interventions in each of the main areas of social protection, and with recent adjustment operations induced by financial crisis, has provided some lessons to guide future work. Successful pension reform involves country ownership, flexibility, institution building, adoption of innovations, and sharing of experience. Social funds do well in terms of targeting, impact, sustainability, comparative advantage, and cost, and have shown the importance of community-driven development in achieving impact. In labor markets, vocational education and training perform best when demand-driven. Job placement activities are generally effective and efficient, while labor supply and demand interventions and enterprise restructuring need careful design. Social safety nets are most effective when established before a crisis hits, and their delivery mechanisms should involve communities. The inclusion of social protection measures in the policy mix supported in adjustment operations has contributed to positive social and economic outcomes.

THE CONCEPT OF SOCIAL RISK MANAGEMENT

At the beginning of the new century, it has become clear that, while individual social protection programs can improve people's welfare and reduce poverty, a more holistic approach is needed to make the quantum leaps necessary to lift more poor people in the developing world out of poverty. This Social Protection Strategy Paper reflects this understanding and uses "social risk management," which is consistent with other current approaches to social policy and poverty reduction, as an important conceptual framework for the World Bank's work in this sector.

The concept of social risk management asserts that individuals, households, and communities are exposed to multiple risks from different sources, both natural (such as earthquakes, floods, and illness) and manmade (such as unemployment, environmental degradation, and war). Poor people are typically more exposed to risk and have less access to effective risk management instruments than people with greater assets and endowments. This vulnerability makes individuals risk-averse and unwilling or unable to engage in high-risk/return activities. Under these circumstances, poor people have developed elaborate mechanisms of "self-protection" such as asset accumulation in good times, diversification of income sources, and creation of informal family and community "risk-pooling" arrangements. However, these arrangements are often relatively expensive and inefficient, and the coping strategies available once a shock occurs often reduce poor people's human capital (for example, cutting back on meals or pulling children out of school to help generate income). This gives rise to the need for public intervention.

Several key concepts are important to an understanding of social risk management. Dealing with risks involves recognizing their sources and economic characteristics, for example, whether they affect individuals in an unrelated manner or simultaneously. The most appropriate combination of risk management strategies (prevention, mitigation, and coping) and arrangements (informal, market-based, and publicly provided or mandated) in any given situation will depend on the type of risk and on the costs and effectiveness of the available instruments. There are also many different sources of risk management instruments (families, communities, nongovernmental organizations [NGOs], market institutions, and government agencies) and varying levels of demand from different groups (such as formal sector workers and lifetime poor people).

All these factors need to be taken into account in designing appropriate risk management strategies for a given population. A clear assessment of a risk management system for any population is possible by examining the available risk management instruments in a matrix of strategies and arrangements—a risk management framework. The World Bank proposes several principles to guide the application of this new framework, including (a) viewing social protection issues in the context of social risk management, (b) looking at all aspects of social protection, (c) achieving a balance among strategies, (d) achieving a balance among arrangements, (e) matching instruments to risks, (f) being prepared for risk, (g) matching supply and demand of risk management instruments, and (h) involving stakeholders in designing and implementing programs.

IMPLICATIONS AND STRATEGY

Based on the social risk management framework, the World Bank, in collaboration with partners, will work to convince policymakers of the importance of risk management to poverty reduction. The World Bank stands ready to offer support in implementing specific social protection instruments or working with other sectors to improve their programs' effect on risk management. This process will be demand-driven and characterized by joint learning and pilot programs in many areas where global knowledge is still limited. In other areas, the World Bank has well-tested products to offer to interested policymakers (for example, in pension reform and support for community-driven development through social funds). For yet another set of interventions, the World Bank will either build on others' experience using its comparative advantage in linking up with the overall macropolicies or help to scale up other agencies' pilot efforts. The World Bank will also continue its practice of supporting partners' efforts when its partners possess the comparative advantage (for example, in child labor).

The social risk management framework applies to many areas of the World Bank's work beyond the social protection sector. Table 1 summarizes how the World Bank can apply social risk management in other areas. If appropriate policies are

x

in place, then households will be much less vulnerable and will be able to smooth their consumption patterns to a degree. This points toward a need to build greater awareness of the significance of risk reduction for the development process. Furthermore, social risk management can serve as an analytical tool to assess interventions in various sectors.

Table 1: Applying Social Risk Management to the World Bank's Work Beyond Social Protection

Areas of World Bank Work	Strategic Directions for the World Bank Using a Social Risk Management Approach
National shocks (economic crises, natural disasters, and civil conflicts)	■ Encourage governments to adopt preventive policies including low inflation ■ Share operational knowledge with disaster management and rural development sectors ■ Support other sectors in developing and piloting appropriate insurance products
The financial sector	■ Promote inclusion of risk management elements in the design of financial sector interventions
Rural development	■ Cooperate in analyzing, piloting, and monitoring innovative ways to manage rural risk
Infrastructure	■ Help relevant sectors to include risk management in analysis of investments
Health, nutrition, population, and education	■ Support development of an integrated human development strategy, emphasizing risk management and human capital development ■ Pursue joint work in areas such as health savings and insurance mechanisms, risk reduction through nutrition programs, early childhood development, multi-sectoral HIV management
Gender issues	■ Promote legal literacy, encourage equal access to productive resources, and ensure equity in access to education and public services

Within the social protection sector itself the risk management framework poses challenges in terms of rethinking existing public sector programs and expanding the range of interventions to provide better support for informal and market-based activities. In the traditional areas of public social protection, reassessment of risk reduction measures (mainly in the area of labor markets) will involve, among other things:

■ Enhancing pre- and in-service skills building. This will entail reorienting the World Bank's approach to ensure access (especially for women) to skills building and to reflect the increasing importance of market-driven training and the shift from skills to knowledge; piloting new training approaches; and reworking existing projects to fit the new framework. This will be done in partnership with international organizations, especially the International Labor Organization (ILO) and interested bilateral donors.

■ Eliminating harmful child labor. Removing children from school is a common coping mechanism for poor households, but it endangers the long-term potential of the children. Some areas of child labor are so clearly harmful that a major global effort should focus on their eradication. The World Bank Group (including the International Finance Corporation [IFC]) will build on its existing approach in this area, continuing to follow the lead of the United Nations Children's Fund (UNICEF) and the ILO.

■ Assisting governments in making labor markets more equitable and inclusive. Because labor is often poor people's main or only asset, equitable access to safe and well-paid work—"decent work" according to the ILO (1999)—is one of the most important aspects of risk reduction. This is reflected in basic labor standards, including the prohibition of forced labor as well as gender and other forms of discrimination in employment and pay. Private or market-based standards, which range from corporate bench-marking and codes of conduct to voluntary enforcement of industry standards, are a promising complement to public labor standards. The World Bank group is actively pursuing these initiatives with several private sector partners.

In terms of risk mitigation, the new strategic directions in the social protection sector will include:

■ Improving old-age income security. In the area of pension systems for the formal sector, the World Bank has become an established leader in conceptual and operational aspects of reform. This began with its development of a flexible approach to old-age security focusing on a "multipillar" system that many countries throughout the world are successfully implementing. While maintaining this approach, the main challenges will be to ensure adequate retirement income for informal sector workers and lifetime poor people, as well as for particularly vulnerable groups such as widows, by strengthening their access to earnings, savings, and other assets.

■ Providing appropriate unemployment benefits. Many developing countries are rightly questioning the standard insurance approach to mitigating the risk of unemployment. The World Bank proposes to assess carefully the experience of alternative instruments (including their gender impact) and pilot them where there is sufficient interest, in close collaboration with the ILO.

Risk coping strategies mainly involve safety nets. Under a social risk management approach, promising avenues relate to interventions that help poor people cope while reducing or mitigating future risks (for example, transfers linked to keeping children in school). Key strategic questions include:

■ How can the social protection sector sustain its support for safety net design and implementation? Resources will be allocated to support impact evaluations while lending will be as responsive as possible (especially in crisis situations).

■ What is the appropriate balance in supporting different types of safety net programs? The World Bank, in partnership with the regional development banks and the International Monetary Fund (IMF), will systematically collect and analyze information on program experience to provide the best possible advice to client countries.

■ How much is enough? While the global financial crisis has emphasized the need for coping programs, care must be taken to ensure that they remain appropriately sized and do not hamper other forms of risk management. Such issues must enter the World Bank's dialogue with the IMF in crisis situations.

■ How can coping interventions help with risk mitigation and reduction? From the perspective of the social risk management framework, this relates to how assistance can be provided in a way that not only increases current levels of consumption for poor women and men but also enables them to manage risk better and climb out of poverty.

As the social protection sector of the World Bank increases its support for government efforts to improve and expand informal risk management mechanisms, it proposes to build on the World Bank's existing experience in the following areas:

■ Rethinking social funds. Social funds have been successful in supporting communities in more than 50 countries. Considering its increased emphasis on community-driven development, the World Bank will support social funds to (a) expand the menu of eligible projects, (b) target vulnerability in addition to poverty, (c) strengthen means to enhance the flow of services from installed infrastructure, and (d) explore further how to ensure that the voices of women and other marginalized groups are better heard in the selection of priorities.

■ Encouraging expansion of support for legal reform efforts. This will ensure that these efforts incorporate measures to strengthen and protect poor people's rights to assets, which includes the review of inheritance laws. Women's property rights are of special concern in many contexts. Reforms should also cover civil law, particularly with respect to women's rights in marriage and divorce.

■ Supporting community-based coping related to orphans and AIDS victims. Efforts will begin in parts of Sub-Saharan Africa where traditional coping mechanisms have come under unbearable strain and will build on the existing activities to support AIDS coping. Women are particularly vulnerable as they are expected to bear the burden of caring for the sick and may face additional social exclusion compared to men.

   The World Bank also has much experience in supporting market-based reforms. The challenge will be to incorporate risk management aspects as much as possible into these reforms without distorting the important moves toward fiscal and financial sustainability. Two areas stand out as potentially promising:

■ Rethinking microfinance within social protection programs. Recent trends in microfinance (toward instruments such as microsavings and microinsurance) and the combination of community-based and market-based arrangements (reinsurance) should provide the chance to develop new models that may meet both financial and social sustainability criteria.

■ Building financial literacy. Because safe financial assets are key to poor people's ability to mitigate risk, there is a potential role for social protection interventions in bridging the gap between formal financial sector reforms and traditional social protection programs (for example, through the promotion of financial literacy).

STRATEGIC DIRECTIONS AND CONCLUSION

The final chapter of this paper summarizes strategic directions for the World Bank's work under the new social protection strategy along the following dimensions: regional and country priorities; traditional Bank products; partnerships with other organizations; and resources (financial and human).

   The paper outlines strategic reorientation in regional work program priorities and countries of emphasis. All regions are proposing to work toward a more holistic approach to risk management, while the detailed work program priorities reflected in the regional sector strategies will depend on the different starting points of the regions, as shown in Table 2.

   Within regional work programs there will be country priorities. An initial determination of countries of emphasis relies on two dimensions: (a) the importance of the country's risk management issues from a global perspective and the comparative advantage of the World Bank relative to other partners in a country; and (b) the opportunity for World Bank involvement (for

Table 2: The World Bank's Social Protection Priorities by Region

Region	Strategic Directions
Sub-Saharan Africa	Work with other human development sectors to mainstream work on orphans and AIDS/HIV management; other sectors to mainstream community-driven development. Integrate pensions and labor work more fully with the rest of social protection.
East Asia and the Pacific	Help clients to establish sustainable public safety nets, improve functioning of and access to market-based arrangements, and review and support informal safety net arrangements.
Europe and Central Asia	Push strongly on second-generation reforms, better integrate social protection subsectors and establish more community-based activities as complement to public interventions.
Latin America and the Caribbean	Integrate social risk management into country dialogue, with country papers helping to identify gaps and need for reform of risk management instruments.
Middle East and North Africa	Improve the functioning of public provisions, the quality of services, and the synergy between governments and civil society in providing social risk management instruments.
South Asia	Establish social risk management as an important element of poverty reduction; focus on microfinance, microinsurance and pension reform in terms of operations.

example, interest of the government in addressing social protection issues). Of special interest in this context are "engagement" countries, which have great global importance but little interest in World Bank involvement; "high-intensity" countries, which are of global significance and possess great interest; and "regional priority" countries, which are of less global importance but which maintain high interest. The categorization of countries is dynamic and will be updated as situations change.

Sub-Saharan Africa (AFR) possesses special challenges. The risks are numerous, severe, and widespread, while the means and instruments for risk management are limited. This indicates a need for a special emphasis on the region. However, three constraints limit the opportunity for the sector:
■ Issues of vulnerability "compete" with other priorities in the region.
■ Where management of vulnerability and risks is identified as a priority, nonsocial protection instruments may provide the best means of dealing with the major risks faced by poor people—for example, droughts, civil war, and disease.
■ The capacity to implement social protection instruments is so low that even if a social protection instrument would work best in an ideal world, the costs of providing social protection in reality may be prohibitively high.

In terms of its traditional product lines (country strategy work, analytical and advisory services, portfolio management, knowledge management, lending, information/communication, and evaluation), the World Bank will promote shifts in strategy consistent with the social risk management approach. In some areas it will also undertake specific actions to reorient its product lines to take full advantage of the new approach, as summarized in Table 3.

Because this strategy paper will expand the World Bank's involvement in social protection, it will be important for the World Bank to reassess its partnerships with other organizations involved in this sector. In this regard, the paper examines partnerships along three dimensions: content, level of cooperation, and type of partner. The World Bank will continually

Table 3: Changes in World Bank Products Based on the New Social Protection Approach

Product	Shifts in Strategy Required by Social Risk Management Approach-Strategic Directions
Country strategy work	■ Promote risk management as a theme in the overall discussion of poverty reduction ■ Use tools such as the social protection PRSP Sourcebook to encourage the incorporation of social protection instruments into country strategies
Analytical and advisory services	■ Move to more comprehensive and action-oriented sector analyses ■ Improve dynamic vulnerability aspects of poverty assessments, especially from a gender perspective
Portfolio management and quality enhancement	■ Maintain the sector's portfolio in a quality leadership position ■ Evaluate the explosive growth in lending, and rework existing operations against the new risk management benchmark
Knowledge management	■ Expand and maintain reform "primers," which compile current analytical thinking, operational lessons and case studies into an accessible handbook format ■ Explore new dissemination technologies
Lending	■ Undertake more piloting ■ Employ adjustment operations in countries still in need of first-generation sector reform and initiate second-generation reforms ■ Scale up community-driven development based on social funds
Information and communication	■ Support dissemination of the new risk management and social protection approach, including through the World Development Report 2000/1 and the World Bank Institute
Evaluation	■ Refine evaluation criteria and benchmarks ■ Adjust household surveys to better reflect vulnerability indicators, including intra-household data ■ Assess the appropriateness of different risk management instruments

review and adjust its interaction with international partners, carefully measuring the costs and benefits of each partnership to allow prioritization and to ensure the selection of those with the highest potential impact on poor people relative to their cost.

The proposed sector strategy, if fully implemented, would imply additional resource requirements. Experience from other sectors with similar rapid growth indicates that the social protection sector needs to make management of the existing portfolio its highest priority. In a low- or no-growth resource scenario, the focus will be on maintaining the quality of the portfolio and supporting implementation of the poverty reduction strategy papers in key heavily indebted countries. With an increase in resources, priority would be given to upstream work for country assistance strategies in non-heavily indebted poor countries, using the basic risk management framework and a revised sourcebook from the poverty reduction strategy work. Gradually, there would be expansion into new activities in support of traditional social protection interventions and into the new areas identified in this strategy. In terms of human resources, this implies a greater need for a broad-based social protection staff, with a few highly specialized staff in key implementation areas.

The strategy outlined in this paper will help the World Bank to be a credible partner in worldwide social policy. As it recently did in the Global Social Summit in Geneva in June 2000 (a five-year review of the Copenhagen Summit of 1995), and its follow-on activities, in the coming years the World Bank will play a key role in important events and processes including the discussion of social protection at the February 2001 session of the United Nations Commission for Social Development and work on the dissemination and application of the World Development Report 2000/1. The next stage of this strategy, developing partnerships involving a common approach to social policy and poverty reduction, will be the true test of whether there will ever be a day when the World Bank's mission statement becomes a reality:

Our dream is a world free of poverty.

AFR	Sub-Saharan Africa Region (World Bank)
AIDS	Acquired Immunodeficiency Syndrome
APEC	Asia Pacific Economic Cooperation
ASEM	Asia-Europe Meeting
CAS	Country Assistance Strategy (World Bank)
CDD	Community-Driven Development (World Bank)
CDF	Comprehensive Development Framework (World Bank)
EAP	East Asia and Pacific Region (World Bank)
ECA	Europe and Central Asia Region (World Bank)
EU	European Union
FY	Fiscal Year
FYR	Former Yugoslav Republic
GDP	Gross Domestic Product
HIPC	Heavily Indebted Poor Country
HIV	Human Immunodeficiency Virus
HNP	Health, Nutrition, and Population (World Bank)
ICFTU	International Confederation of Free Trade Unions
ICT	Information and Communications Technology
IDA	International Development Association
IFC	International Finance Corporation
ILO	International Labor Organization
IMF	International Monetary Fund
ISSA	International Social Security Association
LAC	Latin America and Caribbean Region (World Bank)
MENA	Middle East and North Africa Region (World Bank)
NGO	NonGovernmental Organization
OECD	Organization for Economic Cooperation and Development
OED	Operations Evaluation Department (World Bank)
PAYG	Pay-As-You-Go
PDR	People's Democratic Republic (Laos)
PROST	Pension Reform Options Simulation Toolkit (World Bank)
PRSP	Poverty Reduction Strategy Paper (World Bank, IMF)
SAR	South Asia Region (World Bank)
SIF	Social Investment Fund
SP	Social Protection
SRM	Social Risk Management
UNAIDS	Joint United Nations Program on HIV/AIDS
UNDP	United Nations Development Program
UNICEF	United Nations International Children's Education Fund
WBI	World Bank Institute (World Bank)
WCL	World Confederation of Labor
WDR	World Development Report (World Bank)
WHO	World Health Organization

SOCIAL PROTECTION

AND THE WORLD BANK

For decades, public policy has been concerned with risk and vulnerability associated with factors such as natural disasters, crop failure, war and violence, illness and injury, old age and death, and job loss and business failure. In the development arena, these topics have received increased attention in recent times for at least three reasons:

- Globalization of trade in goods, services, and factors of production and the increased interconnectivity of economies and societies present enormous opportunities for developing countries to prosper. However, globalization also brings new risks and increases the number of possible outcomes.
- Technological change helps to accelerate the pace of development, but at the same time it tends to widen the gulf between the "haves" and the "have-nots," both within and among countries.
- Increased political openness improves governance by holding those in power more accountable to larger segments of the population. As a result, poor people are finding their voices and asking for help in managing the risks that they face.

In this context, the World Bank has developed its first sector strategy for social protection. This process has offered it the opportunity to take stock of experience and develop the strategic thrust of future work. It has also allowed the World Bank to rethink the concept of social protection and embed the analysis, design, and implementation of social protection programs in an integrated poverty reduction framework.

Social protection is one of the youngest of the World Bank's sector groups, coming together in its current configuration only in 1996 with the establishment of the Human Development Network. It is also one of the most dynamic and best performing sectors, with recent high growth in lending and analytical work stimulated by the increased emphasis that countries have given to social issues and by recent financial crises.

This chapter covers the World Bank's involvement in social protection, which began long before the formal establishment of the sector, and reviews the growth and current status of the sector's work program. It also examines the main lessons of social protection operations and programs from current assessments of experience. Based on this analysis, the chapter concludes that it is necessary to adopt a new conceptualization of social protection that is better aligned with current worldwide realities

and emerging thinking about poverty reduction and development.

THE WORLD BANK'S INVOLVEMENT IN SOCIAL PROTECTION—A BRIEF HISTORY

The creation of the modern welfare state, starting modestly in a few industrialized countries toward the end of the nineteenth century, received a boost with the "New Deal" in the United States in the 1930s and emerged fully in Organization for Economic Cooperation and Development (OECD) economies and Eastern Europe after World War II.[1] Many developing countries also introduced social protection measures such as safety nets (often, however, with poor coverage for the most vulnerable) as well as pension schemes, unemployment benefits, and health insurance for formal sector workers.

The World Bank's involvement in social protection began later and on a limited scale but gained momentum in the 1980s. The earliest efforts concentrated on labor markets research and policy work (see Horton, Kanbur, and Mazumdar 1994) and on social protection components of integrated rural development projects. The crises during the 1980s in Latin America and Africa, and the resulting World Bank-supported structural adjustment programs, brought social and human dimensions to the center of the development debate. Many agencies expressed concern that macroeconomic stabilization and structural adjustment were adversely affecting the welfare of poor people (see United Nations International Children's Education Fund [UNICEF] 1987). As a result, social protection instruments became a part of the World Bank's highly visible structural adjustment programs, although they remained mainly reactive and palliative in nature. Some programs, such as social funds, later evolved into free-standing social protection instruments that help poor people deal with a variety of risks, not only those induced by an adjustment program.

The experience of the 1980s led to the production of the *World Development Report 1990* on poverty, which identified the most critical elements of poverty reduction as labor-intensive growth, investment in human capital, and safety nets for poor people. However, safety nets were still viewed as a "last resort"—reactive instruments dealing with the consequences of poverty but not its underlying causes. In this sense, safety net programs represented a cost to be minimized as opposed to an investment for which impact should be maximized.

The quest for growth remained paramount to the World Bank's poverty reduction strategy of the early 1990s, based on the firm notion that more use of the market and better government was the preferred way forward. The idea that growth should be labor-intensive was prominent in the debate, but labor market discussions typically focused on the need to remove distortions and promote macropolicies to achieve this objective. This view increasingly came under pressure through factors such as the inclusion of new member countries after the collapse of communism, repeated crises, and an increasing population share of elderly in developing countries. As a result, the view of social protection expanded gradually, as reflected, for example, in the *World Development Report 1995* on labor issues, which set the stage for the World Bank's "rediscovery" of labor issues and introduced concepts such as core labor standards and the reduction of child labor.

With the collapse of communism and the opening up of Central and Eastern Europe and the former Soviet Union in the early 1990s, social protection programs came to the forefront of the World Bank's work in the region. Both the World Bank and the International Monetary Fund (IMF) found themselves confronted by the ultimate (and fiscally unsustainable) welfare states, which had assumed all risk management and ensured cradle-to-grave security. The need to reduce spending on

these (presumably) nonproductive transfer programs and free up funds for more productive purposes drove the World Bank's initial attempts to address social protection in the new member countries. This was based on the assumption that the transition would be quick, that strong growth (à la East Asia) would take place, and that the main point should be to ensure that expenditures on social protection did not strain the budget. Soon, however, the World Bank and the IMF recognized the importance of targeted transfers to the early losers in the transition and broader social safety nets to cushion the effects of transition.[2]

The first half of the 1990s also brought a series of financial market and policy-induced crises, especially in Latin America and Africa (for example, the peso crisis and the debt crisis). Moreover, the falling relative price of the main export earners in Africa induced an almost constant crisis that disabled growth prospects in large parts of the continent. By this time, in both regions, the response from the World Bank and other multilateral agencies regularly incorporated measures to alleviate both the impact of the crisis and any negative short-term effects of the adjustment measures. Social funds became prevalent throughout much of Latin America, and African countries implemented them as well. India, Bangladesh, and several other Asian countries either expanded or adopted public works programs,[3] and the range of safety net programs also began to widen in other regions, often with an emphasis on food subsidies.

With a rising number of developing countries passing through the demographic transition, support for the elderly became an increasingly important issue in social protection. The World Bank took the lead in the field with the production of a seminal book on pension reform, *Averting the Old Age Crisis* (World Bank 1994), which highlighted the need to manage pension systems proactively while balancing equity, efficiency, fiscal, and financial objectives. The World Bank's program support for pension reform has expanded substantially since this time, especially in Latin America and Eastern Europe (see Annex A).[4]

During the 1990s, social policy in general received a higher profile, culminating with a 1995 summit in Copenhagen that firmly identified social policy and social protection as cornerstones of development (see Box 1.1). Although this represented an advance, there was still relatively little discussion in Copenhagen about informal or market-based solutions. The model that had evolved in the more developed world continued to dominate the

2

debate, even though it was under increasing pressure even in the richest countries.

Most recently, the global financial crisis that first hit East Asia and then Russia and Brazil in 1997-1998 also helped establish social protection as one of the critical elements of a sustainable poverty reduction strategy. The social and poverty implications of the shock and the ramifications of the proposed corrective measures were central and fundamental concerns in the World Bank's quick response to the East Asia crisis. As a result, social

protection interventions constituted an integral part of the overall adjustment programs, as in the case of the emergency support operations for the Republic of Korea (World Bank 1998, 2000c).

The Human Immunodeficiency Virus/Acquired Immune Deficiency Symdrome (HIV/AIDS) pandemic is also causing development planners to broaden their thinking on social protection. In addition to the obvious human tragedy, HIV/AIDS is placing a tremendous strain on the economic and social fabric of the most affected societies, principally through the decimation of the labor supply. It creates additional burdens for women, who are frequently expected to sacrifice their educational and economic aspirations to care for the sick and dying, may be more frequently ostracized and even forced to leave the community when infected, and in some cases may lose their property when their husbands and other male relatives have died.

These recent crises have shown that growth and good macroeconomic policies, while of great importance, are not sufficient for sustained poverty reduction. Shock-resistant risk management programs, including safety nets, income support systems for the elderly, and well-functioning labor markets with social safeguards, are essential to reduce poverty over the long term and protect previous gains. They are necessary for humanitarian reasons and in light of sound economic rationale—the avoidance of long-term poverty can reduce the need for social assistance. The crises have also demonstrated the importance of empowering citizens by encouraging broad participation in decisionmaking.

THE SOCIAL PROTECTION PORTFOLIO AND ANALYTICAL WORK

These external events have been a factor in the seven-fold increase in the World Bank's lending in the social protection area since 1992. The lending volume in FY99 was US$3.76 billion (13 percent of total World Bank lending), up from about US$0.3-0.7 billion in the FY92-FY95 period (Chart 1.1). Policy-based lending has increased (for example, in the large loans to Russia, Korea, Thailand, Indonesia, Argentina, and Brazil), and in FY99, more than 80 percent of social protection lending was in the form of adjustment loans. While the response to the global financial crisis has driven much of the recent rise in lending, the annual lending level for investment operations is about $1/2$ to $3/4$ of a billion dollars, and the World Bank has lent another billion dollars annually in the last three to four years (with wide fluctuations, depending on the size of the

---

BOX 1.1

THE COPENHAGEN SOCIAL SUMMIT AND 20/20 INITIATIVE

The Global Social Summit in Copenhagen in 1995 put social policy at the center of the development debate. The final Copenhagen Declaration and the Program of Action highlighted a number of areas related to social protection. Of the ten "commitments" called for in the Program of Action, Commitment 2 called for the formulation or strengthening of national policies and strategies to reduce inequalities and eradicate absolute poverty by a target date to be set by each country. At the national level, governments were to develop and implement policies "to ensure that all people have adequate economic and social protection during unemployment, ill health, maternity, child-rearing, widowhood, disability, and old age." Commitment 4 fostered social integration "based on the promotion and protection of all human rights, as well as non-discrimination, tolerance, respect for diversity, equality of opportunity, solidarity, security, and participation of all people." This included ensuring "the protection and full integration into the economy and society of disadvantaged and vulnerable groups and persons."

The 20/20 Initiative was part of the Copenhagen Conference and has since gained a life of its own, most recently with an October 1998 follow-up meeting in Hanoi. The goals of this initiative are to ensure that countries and donors each allocate at least 20 percent of their spending or aid flows to social sectors, with 20 percent of this amount directed to primary services. While social protection interventions were not originally present in the 20/20 framework, they are now entering into the discussions.

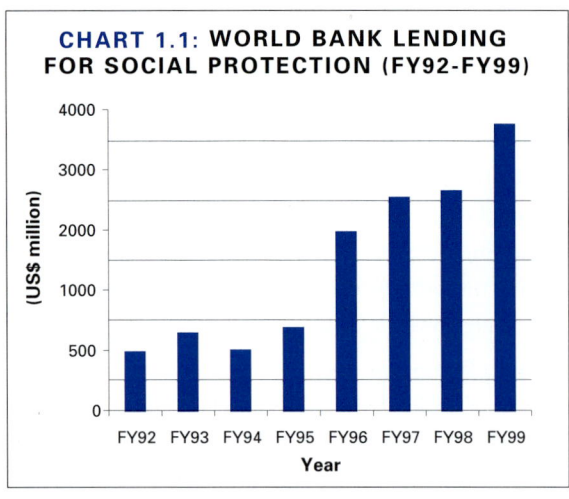

CHART 1.1: WORLD BANK LENDING FOR SOCIAL PROTECTION (FY92-FY99)

Source: World Bank data

countries included in any given year) for noncrisis social protection reform.

In FY99, the social protection portfolio contained 92 loans financing only social protection activities, with a commitment of US$6 billion. Most of these lending operations are in Eastern Europe and Central Asia (ECA), Africa, and Latin America and the Caribbean (LAC). Approximately half of the loans are for social funds and social assistance projects; one-fifth for labor market projects; and the balance for pensions, social insurance, and adjustment operations. An additional 183 loans contained social protection components, adding US$8.9 billion in commitments (making an overall social protection portfolio of US$14.9 billion). In this broader definition of the portfolio, almost two-thirds of commitments (in dollar terms) are for labor market and employment activities, 20 percent for pensions and social insurance, and the balance for social assistance and social funds.

The lion's share of FY91-99 lending went to Latin America and the Caribbean (US$5.46 billion, or 36 percent of the total), East Asia and the Pacific (EAP) (US$3.75 billion, or 25 percent), and Europe and Central Asia (US$2.87 billion, or 19 percent). South Asia, and the Middle East and North Africa (MENA) had the smallest amounts of lending, with 15 and 36 projects approved, respectively, amounting to US$880.7 million and US$984.6 million. Africa had the largest number of projects in the FY91-99 period (95 in total), with a lending volume of US$1.27 billion.

Since the social protection portfolio is relatively young, and a large portion of its lending is in the form of components in projects from other sectors, the World Bank's

Operations Evaluations Department (OED) has provided relatively scarce analysis on its quality or effectiveness. The available evidence indicates that, despite growth in the volume of work without corresponding growth in resources, the sector still maintains better than average quality on the measures commonly used in the World Bank, although some strains are beginning to show:

- The FY99 Annual Portfolio Performance Review found that 14 percent of social protection projects were "at risk" of not meeting their objectives (as measured by the Quality Assurance Group), slightly better than the World Bank-wide average of 19 percent. This indicator improved slightly in FY00, dropping to 13 percent.
- Within the social protection sector, labor market and employment projects generally have the highest levels of "at-risk" rankings, but commitments "at risk" have been concentrated in adjustment operations, mainly loans made to high-risk countries (primarily Russia). By the end of FY00, the situation had improved considerably. Only 5 percent of social protection commitments are currently considered at risk.
- Despite the increase in lending, the social protection sector maintained its high "quality-at-entry" ratings in both 1998 and 1999, with 88 percent and 90 percent satisfactory or better ratings, respectively, slightly above the overall World Bank average.
- The "quality of supervision" remains an area where social protection appears to be below World Bank averages, although 25 percent of social protection projects were rated as highly satisfactory on average for the last two years, compared to a World Bank average of 14 percent.
- There is also some concern that the issue of gender discrimination in labor markets, property rights, access to productive resources, and income support has not yet been fully addressed in many contexts.

Although the Operations Evaluation Department has not done an overall evaluation of the social protection portfolio, it has reviewed the World Bank's Implementation Completion Reports for a number of social protection projects. In general, social protection projects had an 86 percent satisfactory rating in 1999, but sustainability was deemed to be uncertain in more than 70 percent of the projects. This appears to be based mainly on an assumption that the social fund agencies will not be maintained beyond the lifetime of the projects. However, independent impact evaluations have indicated that projects financed by the agencies are

4

sustainable and have higher usage rates than similar investments (Jorgensen and Van Domelen 2000; Rawlings, Sherburne-Benz, and Van Domelen 2000).

The sector's analytical work has grown in parallel with and, in some cases, in advance of the rapid rise in the World Bank's lending. As indicated above, the World Bank has done major analytical work on safety nets (World Bank 1990), pensions (World Bank 1994), and labor markets (World Bank 1995). More recently, the World Bank has begun to produce a Pension Reform Primer series—a comprehensive toolkit for policymakers and World Bank staff on designing and implementing pension reform—to provide much needed "how-to" advice to practitioners. The World Bank's safety net/social funds and labor markets thematic groups are preparing similar toolkits for their subsectors. More traditional World Bank country reports, such as Country Economic Memoranda, Poverty Assessments, Social Sector Reviews, Public Expenditure Reviews, and specific sector reports on social protection topics have also been used to provide advice in this area to the World Bank's client countries (see Annex B).

Various World Bank units have been actively involved in generating and disseminating information related to social protection. The Development Economics research group has done studies on labor market policies and institutions; public sector downsizing; income support programs for the unemployed, the administrative and political economy aspects of pension reform, health, pensions and aging; the decentralization of social assistance; child labor; and private transfers. The World Bank Institute runs a number of training events for policymakers and practitioners, including an annual two-week course with Harvard University on pension reform, a core course on pensions, global and regional workshops on social funds, and a series of training activities for personnel from countries in the former Soviet Union.

EMERGING LESSONS OF SOCIAL PROTECTION OPERATIONS AND PROGRAMS

The social protection and poverty reduction groups in the World Bank and other agencies have carried out a number of assessments of experiences with different forms of social protection interventions. A number of lessons are emerging from the portfolio in each main social protection area (pensions, social funds, labor markets, and social safety nets) and in financial crisis-induced adjustment operations.

The reform of public pension systems has been an important area of activity for the social protection sector. The World Bank has been formally involved in 70 technical assistance, project, and reform loans in 36 countries during the past 15 years (for more details, see Annex A). While the growing deficit of an unfunded pension scheme is the usual trigger for reform, the need to address this fiscal problem goes well beyond pension concerns, since pension deficits typically crowd out other (often poverty-oriented) social expenditures on, for instance, education, health, and social safety nets. To put the public scheme on a financially sustainable base often proves to be a lengthy and protracted operation. Key ingredients for success[5] include:

- Country ownership of the reforms. This involves commitment and consensus building among the main groups in the population, information campaigns, credible fiscal and benefit projections, a political reform champion, and other elements of the political economy of reform.
- Flexibility in the reform approach. While the World Bank's proposed multipillar approach to pensions continues to be a useful benchmark, it is not a blueprint, and any reform has to take account of a country's starting conditions and preferences.
- Institution building. Changing the law is only the first step; major support for institution building is necessary to make the reform successful and sustainable. For the World Bank's operations, this means supplementing reform loans with investment and technical assistance operations.
- Working with the government on innovations. Since there is no fixed recipe for reform, the government and the World Bank must be innovative in order to address many of the open problems of pension reform implementation, which include containing administrative costs, providing annuities, and strengthening information technology.
- Sharing experience. While each country has its own reform approach, the dissemination of cross-country experience has proven to be a major vehicle to accelerate reforms and make them successful. To this end, the World Bank has an important role to play through the activities of the World Bank Institute, the elaboration of Pension Reform Primer series, and cooperation with other international institutions involved in this area such as the ILO, OECD, Asian Development Bank, and Inter-American Development Bank (IADB).

5

Assessments of social funds have, until recently, been mainly desk reviews or partial assessments at best. An Inter-American Development Bank evaluation of social funds did show generally positive results, but it was not based on household data (Goodman and others 1997). The social protection sector has sponsored two assessments of social funds to provide a more complete picture. First, there was a review of all beneficiary assessments (Owen and Van Domelen 1998), which found that, in general, social fund interventions responded well to expressed community demands and that there was general satisfaction among stakeholders with the impact of the investments.

In 1998, the World Bank began the second study, the Social Funds 2000 Impact Evaluation study, a major multi-country evaluation of the impact, targeting, and cost-efficiency of social fund interventions coordinated by the social protection and poverty reduction groups. The study is using four types of information: household surveys, facilities surveys, participatory assessments, and administrative data. There are six countries in the study—Armenia, Bolivia, Honduras, Nicaragua, Peru, and Zambia. The preliminary results show evidence in the following areas:[6]

- Targeting. Social fund interventions are normally well targeted, including to people in the poorest income decile.
- Impact. The interventions generally have a positive, sustainable impact.
- Comparative advantage. Social fund-financed schools and clinics tend to be better staffed, better equipped, and in better physical shape than other clinics and schools.
- Costs. Social funds sometimes have lower costs than comparative interventions and sometimes have higher costs, depending on the "completeness" of the investments.

In summary, social funds appear to be a useful, sustainable investment in local-level risk management and social development. However, some areas of debate are how to achieve better integration of the concerns of local government and potential problems resulting from the use of the social fund mechanism, including bypassing line ministries and the diminishing perceived need for sectoral reform. Future research efforts should concentrate on these issues.

The work of the World Bank in labor markets involves many small projects or small labor market components in larger projects (Dar and Tzannatos 1999b). The main areas of social protection operations are vocational training and education (in cooperation with the education sector), active labor market policies, small-scale employment projects, large-scale enterprise restructuring projects, and support for labor market legislation reform. Recently, project work started on child labor programs and labor standards, and analytical work began on activity-oriented labor market reviews. The emerging lessons are as follows:

- Vocational training and education offer rich experience and lessons (Gill, Fluitman, and Dar 2000), but there is not yet a benchmark model of modern pre- and in-service training that the World Bank can credibly offer to its client countries.[7] The main challenge is to find a new role for the government, moving it from traditional and all- encompassing provision of vocational training and education to the (co-)financing and supervision of private sector-provided and/or -sponsored activities.
- The area of active labor market policies has included measures to improve labor supply (for example, through training), labor demand (for example, through wage subsidies), and better balancing of labor supply and demand (for example, through job placement offices and job counseling). A first evaluation of the experience of World Bank projects (Fretwell, Benus, and O'Leary 1999) and of developed countries (Dar and Tzannatos 1999a) provides a differentiated and modestly optimistic outlook. While job placement activities seem to be largely effective and efficient, measures to improve labor supply or demand work best if they are small-scale, targeted to specific groups, and well evaluated and supervised.
- There is no consistent comparison yet available on small-scale employment projects. For large-scale enterprise restructuring, scarce evidence suggests the need to include workers in the restructuring process from the very beginning; to do a careful microeconomic analysis of the existing wage and nonwage compensation when offering compensation packages; and to link restructuring with the opening of private sector job opportunities, which in turn requires putting the reform effort into the broader scope of a country's reform program.

In the area of social safety nets, no complete evaluation is yet available. There are some policy assessments on specific issues such as targeting (Grosh 1994) and at a more general level (Subbarao and others 1997).[8] Existing evidence suggests the following main lessons (see also World Bank 2000f):

- Informal household and community-based mechanisms still account for much of the safety net function. These mechanisms seemingly work for most but not all of the population if the shock is idiosyncratic and not catastrophic, but they fail under a protracted and severe crisis.
- Public safety net provisions in the form of public works and transfer payments in cash or kind work best if they have been established before the crisis hits.
- The delivery of social safety nets is best done through local communities, which provide control and ownership but still require guidelines, supervision, and financial support from the central government.

While large-scale structural adjustment operations in the past have essentially concentrated on macroeconomic financial and fiscal issues, with social safety nets more of an addendum than a loan component, many structural adjustment loans made during the recent East Asia crisis included social protection as a major element (World Bank 1998, 2000c). The Korean Structural Adjustment Loans I and II are among the most important and successful examples. These loans focused on financial sector reform, enterprise restructuring, and social protection, linking all three activities in a coherent and consistent policy matrix. Furthermore, the social protection part included all main subsectors—social insurance (pensions), labor markets, and social safety nets (poverty issues)—and treated them in a consistent manner. The integrated approach of these loans, and their inclusion of all the key social protection areas, helped mitigate the effect of the crisis on poor people.

WHAT DOES THIS ADD UP TO?

Social protection policies and programs, prevalent in developed countries for decades, are finding their way into developing countries. With considerable regional variation, the reform of pension schemes (and other forms of social insurance) and the (de)regulation of labor markets are becoming more common. Also, social assistance and social funds have become a widely used response to protect poor people. Increasingly throughout the 1980s and 1990s, the World Bank has responded to changing global, regional, and country circumstances with analytical, advisory, and lending services in support of these elements of social protection. Starting with highly fragmented, small-scale, reactive interventions, the World Bank has increased the scope and scale of its social protection support to client countries, culminating in the almost fully-integrated response to the countries affected by the East Asian crisis.

We have learned from these experiences that social protection projects and programs are needed and in demand by the World Bank's client countries and have, by and large, been effective. However, as the world has evolved, so has the need for the World Bank to modify its approach to social protection. To date, the increase in operations has occurred largely within the confines of each of the social protection subsectors: (a) the approach toward pension reform has expanded to look at markets and informal actions; (b) social funds have increasingly started to examine causes of poverty and not simply the consequences of structural adjustment; and (c) labor market interventions have begun to address topics such as core labor standards. With the latest interventions and the greater frequency of shocks, this partial, subsector approach is no longer appropriate.

Our experience has shown the need for a new, integrated conceptual framework that builds on previous knowledge but better reflects the world situation at the beginning of the 21st century—a situation where risks and opportunities are on the rise, where it is recognized that neither the state nor the market alone will provide the best solution, and where the plight of more than 1 billion poor people poses the question of how to manage risk better, not merely providing handouts after a shock has occurred. For the World Bank, this implies an even stronger need to incorporate social protection subsectors within an overall framework. It also indicates the urgency of integrating social protection with other sectors and themes at the World Bank.

NOTES FROM CHAPTER ONE

[1] Transfers (income and in-kind "handouts") to poor people have existed for centuries but, historically, the main providers were religious organizations, private benefactors, and sometimes communities.

[2] The IMF program for Poland in 1990 was the first to include a chapter on social safety nets, and World Bank Country Economic Memoranda started to include sections on social programs and labor markets.

7

[3] Many of these public works programs have been around, however, for a very long time. India's public works programs began in the nineteenth century. In Botswana between 1985 and 1986, 21 percent of the labor force participated in public works, while in Chile this figure was around 13 percent in 1985.

[4] For the World Bank's perspective on pension reform, see Holzmann (2000).

[5] See Holzmann (2000).

[6] The Operations Evaluation Department is currently undertaking an assessment, the Social Funds Evaluation, that will use data from ongoing studies, such as the Social Funds 2000 Impact Evaluation Study, to judge the relevance, efficacy, and efficiency of social funds. It will focus, however, on the criteria of sustainability and institutional development (including social capital), using primary data from case studies in four countries (Jamaica, Malawi, Nicaragua, and Zambia).

[7] This is a key strategic priority to help reduce the risk of underemployment or unemployment (Chapter 5).

[8] The East Asia crisis and its aftermath have triggered an enhanced interest in the functioning of safety nets during financial crisis, the lessons to be learned, and the impact of World Bank operations. Under the "APEC Finance Social Safety Net Initiative" the Bank is currently participating with the IMF and Inter-American Development Bank in a fact-finding and lesson-learning exercise that covers six countries in Latin America and East Asia.

THE NEW FRAMEWORK:

SOCIAL RISK MANAGEMENT

"The revolutionary idea that defines the boundary between modern times and the past is the mastery of risk: the notion that the future is more than a whim of gods and that men and women are not passive before nature."
— Peter L. Bernstein (1996)

In preparing a new strategy for the social protection sector, the World Bank needed to formulate a comprehensive yet operational framework linking social protection concepts to the broader agenda of poverty reduction. This chapter describes the new way of looking at social protection based on the concept of social risk management.[1]

WHY A NEW FRAMEWORK?

Traditionally, social protection has been defined by its program components, consisting of labor market interventions (including child labor), social insurance (including pensions), and social safety nets (including social funds). This narrow conceptualization, however, overlooks important aspects of social protection, such as how these programs overlap and interact, and it provides little guidance on how social protection can contribute to effective poverty reduction beyond passive income redistribution. Furthermore, the traditional framework fails to address the distribution of risks and resources within the household as well as gender differences in experiences of poverty and vulnerability.

In its new definition, social protection is seen as public interventions that assist individuals, households, and communities to manage risk better and that provide support to the critically poor. The underlying framework of social risk management has the following features:

■ It regards social protection as a springboard, as well as a safety net, for poor people. While a safety net for all should exist, the programs should also provide poor people with the capacity to climb out of poverty, or at least to resume gainful work. The springboard is particularly important for women, who are subject to socially imposed constraints on their access to productive resources.[2]

■ It regards social protection interventions as investments rather than costs. For example, helping poor people to maintain their access to basic social services during shocks fosters their future productive capacity. On the other hand, merely giving them transfers to cope with the shock may not accomplish the same goal.

■ It focuses less on the symptoms and more on the causes of poverty by making it possible for poor people to engage in activities that have higher risks but also higher returns, and thus to avoid poverty traps.

■ It takes account of reality. Less than a quarter of the world's population has access to formal social protection programs, and less than 5 percent can rely on private assets to manage risk. At the same time, eliminating the poverty gap through public transfers is beyond the fiscal capacity of most countries.

KEY CONCEPTS OF THE NEW FRAMEWORK

The main idea behind social risk management is that all individuals, households, and communities are exposed to multiple risks from different sources, whether they are natural (such as earthquakes, floods, and illness) or manmade (such as discriminatory practices, unemployment, environmental degradation, and war).

Poor people are more vulnerable than other population groups because they are typically more exposed to risk and have little access to appropriate risk management instruments. Being poor, and hence vulnerable, makes individuals very risk-averse, therefore unwilling or unable to engage in high-risk/return activities. Moreover, the coping strategies available to them once a shock occurs are often likely to reduce their human capital (see Box 2.1). In addition to the gender-neutral consequences of poverty, women are also subject to additional socially determined constraints on their ability to manage risk and to escape from poverty.[3]

Several key concepts are critical to an understanding of social risk management. The concept of social risk management differs from the concepts of social protec-

tion and redistribution, although there are areas of overlap. Dealing with risks involves recognizing the source and economic characteristics of the risks; for example, whether they affect individuals in an unrelated manner or simultaneously. The most appropriate combination of risk management arrangements (informal, market-based, or publicly provided or mandated) and risk management strategies (prevention, mitigation, or coping) in any given situation depends on the type of risk and on the costs and effectiveness of the available instruments. Furthermore, risk management instruments come from different suppliers (such as the family, communities, nongovernmental organizations, market institutions, and the government) and need to meet the demands of different groups (for example, formal sector workers and the lifetime poor). These variables lead to a multitude of possible arrangements.

Interactions Among Social Risk Management, Social Protection, and Redistribution

The concept of social risk management overlaps to some extent with the concepts of social protection and income redistribution, but each area of public intervention also has its own space, as shown graphically in Chart 2.1. Determining the boundaries among them depends to some extent on political choices about the scope of public intervention and the function of social policy in society. Hence, the overlaps and boundaries will differ among countries, but common issues remain.

The darkest shaded area in Chart 2.1 represents issues that involve social protection (SP) but are outside the scope of redistribution and social risk management (SRM), such as social inclusion. The medium gray-shaded area represents the intersection of redistribution

10

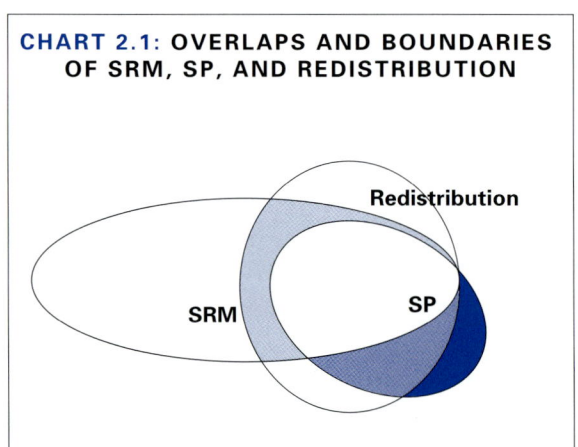

CHART 2.1: OVERLAPS AND BOUNDARIES OF SRM, SP, AND REDISTRIBUTION

Redistribution

SRM

SP

Source: World Bank data

and social protection outside social risk management (such as income support for the critically poor). The unshaded area of SP signifies social protection as part of social risk management. The light-gray-shaded area comprises issues of income redistribution that are part of social risk management but outside social protection (such as targeted infrastructure investments to prevent or mitigate risk). The unshaded area of the redistribution set corresponds to public measures designed solely to achieve more equal income distribution (such as progressive income taxation). Finally, the unshaded area of the social risk management set presents risk management that does not involve social protection (such as sound macroeconomic policy). These concepts and their policy implications are outlined further below.

Social risk management beyond social protection.
Many areas of public policy that affect vulnerability and income variability clearly do not involve social protection. Policymakers often fail to understand fully that sound macroeconomic policy, stable financial markets, enforcement of property rights, respect for basic labor rights, and growth-oriented policies are the first and best ingredients for dealing with risk and enhancing welfare. This suggests an information-sharing role for social protection. The concept of social risk management can also be a powerful analytical instrument to evaluate policy or project measures (for example, structural adjustment or irrigation schemes) on one aspect of their potential poverty reduction impact, namely their risk management effects (see Chapter 4).

Social protection and income redistribution. Income redistribution is an important aspect of social risk management and social protection activities, but unlike traditional social protection or the welfare state, it is not necessarily the primary or only goal. In the social risk management framework, income redistribution is present as an equity objective linked to adverse risk and as an important outcome of good social protection programs. The support of the critically poor is a main objective of social protection. Since financing cash or in-kind transfers requires taxes on workers or nonworking wealthy, income redistribution appears as a result. Also, enhancing risk management capacity has high redistributive effects on individuals' welfare, yet it does not require interpersonal income redistribution to achieve a more equal welfare

distribution. On the other hand, not all redistribution is a form of social protection—redistributive efforts accomplished through a tax-transfer mechanism or through the distributive effects of public goods provision lie outside social protection, for example.

Social protection beyond social risk management and redistribution: social inclusion. Advocates of policies to combat social exclusion argue that modern social protection should not be limited to traditional forms of income support but should include measures to promote social cohesion, solidarity, and inclusion. On the one hand, an income support system for the unemployed may not only enhance individual welfare by reducing vulnerability but also help to achieve social stability. On the other hand, social protection may extend well beyond mere financial and income-oriented considerations. This broader approach would include investments to support informal arrangements and upgrade the nonprofit sector, strengthen the "social rights" aspects of social policy, and extend the view of social risk management to include the broad concept of "social capital" (Badelt 1999).

Promoting social inclusion is an important objective of the World Bank.[4] While the social, cultural, and political determinants of social inclusion may be beyond the scope of social risk management, it is essential to recognize the causes and consequences of social exclusion and to design strategies that address these issues. For example, public works programs in a number of African countries may find it difficult to involve women if they rely on cash payments as opposed to in-kind payments such as food. Similarly, in cultures that limit women's ability to travel, women will not be able to take full advantage of economic opportunities or public services located outside their area of residence.

Sources of Risks and their Characteristics
The capacities of individuals, households, and communities to handle risk, and the choice of risk management instrument, depend on the characteristics of risks: their sources, correlation, frequency, and intensity. The sources of risk may be natural (for example, floods) or the result of human activity (for example, inflation resulting from economic policy); risks can be uncorrelated (idiosyncratic) or correlated among individuals (covariant), over time (repeated), or with other risks (bunched). Risks can involve infrequent but severe welfare effects (catastrophic)

or frequent but low welfare effects (noncatastrophic). Table 2.1 presents main sources of risk and the degree of covariance that can range from purely idiosyncratic (micro), to regionally covariant (meso), to nationwide covariant (macro) events.

While informal or market-based risk management instruments can often handle idiosyncratic risks, they tend to break down when facing highly covariant, macro-type risks. In Africa, for example, the main sources of covariant risks that affect poor people are AIDS, wars and conflict, seasonal volatility in prices, drought, and macro-economic shocks. Idiosyncratic risks include illness and widowhood or the breakup of the family. Since many of the risks faced by poor people are covariant in nature, informal management mechanisms at the family or community level are typically not very effective. Among these risks, at least two are induced by human activity (war and macroeconomic shocks), which need no coping mechanism if they can be prevented from happening in the first place. Access to market-based interventions, such as saving mechanisms or insurance programs, can mitigate some of the risks (seasonal price volatility or illness). This suggests that different strategies and interventions are appropriate depending on the nature of the risks involved.

Table 2.1: Main Sources of Risk

	Micro (Idiosyncratic) ←	Meso	→ Macro (Covariant)
Natural		Rainfall, landslides, volcanic eruption	Earthquakes, floods, drought, strong winds
Health	Illness, injury, disability	Epidemic	
Lifecycle	Birth, old age, death		
Social	Crime, domestic violence	Terrorism, gangs	Civil strife, war, social upheaval
Gender	Control over household resources	Social acceptance of gender violence	Legal discrimination against women
Economic	Business failure	Unemployment Resettlement Harvest failure	Output collapse Balance of payments, Financial or currency crisis Technology- or trade-induced terms of trade shocks
Political	Ethnic discrimination	Riots	Political default on social programs Coup d'état
Environmental		Pollution Deforestation Nuclear disaster	

Source: Adapted from Holzmann and Jorgensen 1999; Sinha and Lipton 1999; World Bank 2000f.

Social Risk Management Arrangements

Over time, different kinds of social risk management arrangements have evolved. These fall into three main categories: (a) informal arrangements, (b) market-based arrangements, and (c) public arrangements on a large scale. Each has relative strengths and limitations.

Informal Arrangements. These arrangements have existed for a long time and still constitute the main source of risk management for the majority of the world's population. In the absence of market institutions and public provision of support, individual households respond to risk by protecting themselves through informal or personal arrangements. Although they side-step most of the information and coordination problems that cause market failure, they may not be very effective in helping the household weather adverse events. Examples of this kind of arrangement include: the buying and selling of real assets (such as cattle, real estate, and gold), informal borrowing and lending, crop and field diversification, the use of safer production technologies (such as growing less risky crops), storing goods for future consumption, mutual community support arrangements, and kinship arrangements through marriage.

Market-Based Arrangements. Individual households will also take advantage of market-based institutions such as money, banks, and insurance companies when they are available. However, in view of these instruments' limitations due to market failure, their usage will be initially restricted but will rise with financial market development. Empirical evidence suggests that the establishment of a sound banking system and noninflationary policy is crucial to reducing and managing risk. Because formal market institutions are reluctant to lend to households without secured earnings, microfinance is also an important instrument of social risk management.

Public Arrangements. Public arrangements for dealing with risk are relatively scarce and have very limited coverage in the developing world for fiscal and other reasons. When informal or market-based risk management arrangements do not exist, break down, or are dysfunctional, the government can provide or mandate (social) insurance programs for risks such as unemployment, old age, work injury, disability, widowhood, and sickness. The mandatory participation in a risk pool can circumvent issues of adverse selection, in which individuals with low-risk profiles avoid participation in insurance pools due to premiums while individuals with high-risk profiles join in order to gain access to payouts. Because these programs typically apply to those in formal employment, their coverage in developing countries is generally low. On the other hand, governments have a whole array of instruments to help households cope after a shock hits, such as social assistance, subsidies on basic goods and services, and public works programs. The measures a government chooses to implement depend on its distributive concerns, its fiscal resources, its administrative capacities, and the type of risk involved.

Social Risk Management Strategies

Risk management can take place at different moments—both before and after the risk occurs. The goal of ex ante measures is to prevent the risk from occurring, or, if this cannot be done, to mitigate its effects. Individual efforts, such as migration, can prevent risks, but in many cases they require government support (for example, disaster prevention). Mitigating the effects of risk through risk pooling by definition requires interaction among individuals, and poor people are typically less able to participate in formal and also informal arrangements. This leaves most poor households with the residual option of coping with the risk once it has occurred. They are normally not well prepared to do this and, therefore, often experience irreversible negative effects. For this reason, there is a great deal of public intervention in risk coping.

Prevention Strategies. These are strategies implemented before a risk event occurs. Reducing the probability of an adverse risk increases people's expected income and reduces income variance, and both of these effects improve welfare. Preventive social protection interventions typically form part of measures designed to reduce risks in the labor market, notably the risk of unemployment, underemployment, or low wages resulting from inappropriate skills or malfunctioning labor markets.

Mitigation Strategies. As with prevention strategies, mitigation strategies aim to address the risk before it occurs. Whereas preventive strategies reduce the probability of the risk occurring, mitigation strategies help individuals reduce the impact of a future risk event through pooling over assets, individuals, and time. For example, households may "pool" uncorrelated risks through informal and formal insurance mechanisms. While formal insurance instruments profit from a large pool of participants, which leads to less correlated risks,

13

informal insurance has the advantage of all participants having access to almost the same amount of information.

Coping Strategies. These strategies are designed to relieve the impact of the risk once it has occurred. The main forms of coping consist of individual dis-saving, borrowing, or relying on public or private transfers. The government has an important role to play when individuals or households have not saved enough to handle repeated or catastrophic risks.

Using Coping, Mitigation, and Risk Reduction Strategies Together. At face value, the best social risk management is to make sure that down-side risks never occur. The next most effective action is risk mitigation, as this reduces the negative effects of risks before they actually happen. Risk coping is essentially the residual strategy if everything else has failed. However, since each of these strategies has both direct and opportunity costs, relying entirely on risk reduction or mitigation may not be either efficient or feasible. The experience of the formerly centrally planned economies has demonstrated that trying to eliminate all risks in advance through quantity planning, official price setting, and public ownership of productive means has serious costs in terms of lower economic growth.

At the other extreme, many of the current government interventions in developing countries, particularly for poor people, concentrate on risk coping. However, a system that concentrates on helping poor people deal with a shock once it has occurred runs the risk of keeping them in a poverty trap and perpetuating the vicious cycle of low returns, low risktaking, and deep poverty. Moving toward a balance among coping, reduction, and mitigation strategies has the potential to trigger a virtuous cycle in which people can undertake activities with higher variability in returns, but also with higher absolute returns.

The accumulation of assets[5] (such as land, cattle, and financial savings) and policies that discourage disinvestment of a detrimental nature (such as cutting down trees) are of the utmost importance in this regard. Equally important are efforts to reduce child labor, enhance the skills of the labor force, involve the local community in projects, widen access to safe financial assets, and design appropriate unemployment benefits. This does not mean that social safety nets should be neglected, since they are clearly necessary, particularly during periods of natural disaster or economic crisis. Rather, it implies that the World Bank could help structure programs that support coping to help reduce risk (for instance, by subsidizing education during a crisis).

THE SOCIAL RISK MANAGEMENT MATRIX

The social risk management framework is a powerful diagnostic and analytical instrument, since it takes into account the different sources and economic characteristics of risks, proposes alternative strategies and arrangements for dealing with risks, and highlights different actors in the supply and demand of risk management instruments. This section develops a social risk management matrix and explains guiding principles for its application.

The social risk management matrix shown in Table 2.2 provides examples of risk management instruments by type of arrangement (informal, market-based, and public) and by strategy (risk reduction, mitigation, and coping). Filling in each cell of the matrix with existing instruments provides a means of examining the status of social risk management in a given country or subgroup within a country. Comparisons can be made among countries to assess differences and to determine appropriate and useful changes in a given country based on opportunity costs and comparative advantage. (See Annex C for application of the matrix to world regions.)

While each cell of the matrix can be filled in most countries, the intensity and scope of application are likely to differ and change over time. The poorest countries will be characterized by a predominance of informal arrangements and public arrangements concentrated on coping strategies. In contrast, richer countries will apply the whole set of public arrangements and strategies, and market-based instruments and strategies geared toward risk mitigation and reduction will grow in importance.

GUIDING PRINCIPLES

What does the new social risk management framework imply for the World Bank's development work in social protection? The following principles have been designed to guide the World Bank's future work in this area. The principles reflect the complexity of the framework and its relevance to social protection, to the World Bank's work in client countries, and to its overarching mission of reducing poverty in the developing world.

View Social Protection in the Context of Social Risk Management

Managing risk with adequate capacity and appropriate interventions is an integral aspect of economic development in general and of poverty reduction in particular.

The concept of social risk management extends well beyond the field of social protection, even though social protection is an important and integral part of social risk management. Approaching social risk management only from the perspective of social protection would mean missing out on many effective and efficient policy actions that could be taken outside the sector. This implies taking a holistic approach in devising interventions that help individuals, households, and communities cope with the risks to which they are exposed. It also makes it necessary for all the relevant sectors to coordinate in designing the appropriate interventions.

Look at all Aspects of Social Protection

In the past, social protection was often viewed merely as the direct public provision of risk management instruments. As a result, the World Bank has done little to try to strengthen the risk management arrangements provided by the market, households, or communities themselves. In the future, the World Bank must take all of these aspects into account in considering the best risk management strategies to recommend in a client country. Taking a broad view of social protection makes it possible to identify the most appropriate mix of institutions and instruments for reducing poverty and supporting

Table 2.2: Strategies and Arrangements of Social Risk Management—Examples

Arrangements and Strategies	Informal	Market-based	Public
Risk Reduction			
	• Less risky production • Migration • Proper feeding and weaning practices • Engaging in hygiene and other disease preventing activities	• In-service training • Financial market literacy • Company-based and market-driven labor standards	• Public labor standards • Pre-service training • Labor market policies • Child labor interventions • Disability policies • Good macroeconomic policies • AIDS and other disease prevention • Legislation to remove gender inequalities in property rights, marriage, and access to labor markets
Risk Mitigation			
Portfolio	• Multiple jobs • Investment in human, physical, and real assets • Investment in social capital (rituals, reciprocal gift-giving)	• Investment in multiple financial assets • Microfinance	• Multipillar pension systems • Asset transfers • Protection of property rights (especially for women) • Support for extending financial markets to poor people
Insurance	• Marriage/family • Community arrangements • Share tenancy • Tied labor	• Old-age annuities • Disability, accident, and other personal insurance • Crop, fire, and other damage insurance	• Mandated/provided insurance for unemployment, old-age, disability, survivorship, sickness, etc.
Risk Coping			
	• Selling of real assets • Migration • Borrowing from neighbors • Intra-community transfers/charity • Sending children to work • Dis-saving in human capital	• Selling of financial assets • Borrowing from banks	• Transfers/social assistance • Subsidies • Public works

economic development given a country's traditions, culture, circumstances, and budget. Also, social protection strategies must recognize and seek to address the legal, economic, political, social, and cultural factors that determine gender differences in exposure to risk and in the effectiveness of risk management strategies.

Achieve a Balance Among Strategies

Historically, risk coping has commanded too much attention; risk mitigation, too little; and risk prevention, even less. Though this may be understandable in view of their comparative direct costs and benefits, it is likely to be inefficient if indirect costs and long-term benefits are taken into account. Reaching an economically determined balance among the three strategies should be advantageous to beneficiaries, particularly poor people, but may be tricky to pull off politically, financially, and conceptually. For example, disaster prevention may reduce costs over the long term, but it is likely to require a high initial budget outlay.

Achieve a Balance Among Arrangements

Informal, market-based, and public arrangements for dealing with risk all have comparative advantages. These are determined by who has information and the capacity to handle it, and by the long-term development implications of each arrangement. While in all countries informal arrangements existed first, some countries (such as the Soviet Union) relied for a time almost entirely on public arrangements. In an ideal world with perfectly symmetrical information and complete, well-functioning markets, all risk management arrangements can and should be market-based (except for the incapacitated). However, in the real world, all risk management arrangements will play important roles that are likely to change over time.

Match Instruments to Risks

Individuals, households, and communities are poorly equipped to handle certain types of risks, including natural disasters, epidemics, and financial meltdowns. These risks require interventions from governments, international institutions, and the world community. In the case of less catastrophic risks, informal and market-based arrangements may be appropriate, but public intervention, such as regulation, mandates, or services, will still be needed in many instances. However, this kind of public intervention must be designed in accordance with the type of risk involved and the environment in which it occurs. The difficult transition from a planned to a market economy in the countries of the former Soviet Union in the 1990s and the recent financial shock in East Asia have highlighted the need for solutions tailored to the problem at hand.

Be Prepared for the Risk

The economic crisis experienced by Latin America in the 1980s and 1990s and the recent East Asia crisis have demonstrated that basic social risk management instruments should be in place before any crisis hits. Once the crisis has occurred, it is very difficult to build political consensus on appropriate policies and establish the necessary institutional frameworks to implement them.

Match the Supply and Demand of Risk Management Instruments

There are many suppliers of risk management instruments (such as individuals, households, communities, nongovernmental organizations, financial markets, governments at different levels, bilateral donors, and international organizations), and there are distinct differences in demand among different population groups (such as formal, informal urban, and informal rural workers). Risk can be adequately addressed only if the applied instruments are well matched to the needs of the relevant group. The role of the government in making this match between supply and demand is complex. Not only should the government provide its own instruments, but it should also increase the supply and effectiveness of instruments from other sources.

Involve Stakeholders in Designing and Implementing Programs

Since the objective of social risk management is to help people and communities manage risk better, the beneficiaries and other stakeholders should ideally be involved in designing and implementing the interventions. This conclusion is supported by evidence from the World Bank's implementation experience, whether in incorporating poor people's own priorities into the design of social funds, opening up the pension reform debate as widely as possible, or consulting with labor market organizations on public sector restructuring programs. Since in many societies community and local decisionmaking is largely in the hands of men, participatory strategies must be designed to ensure that women have a voice in the selection and implementation of strategies.

16

¹ See Holzmann and Jorgensen (1999, 2000) for a more comprehensive presentation of the framework.

[1] See Holzmann and Jorgensen (1999, 2000) for a more comprehensive presentation of the framework.

[2] Studies in Africa have estimated that giving women farmers equal access to productive inputs (for example, reducing their yield risk) could increase their productivity by up to 20 percent. Similarly, lowering the risk of girls not gaining employment by increasing their education levels to those of boys could increase the rate of Gross National Product growth by as much as 50 percent in some African countries (World Bank 2000e, Gender Chapter).

[3] Examples of these constraints include: restricted control over domestic property and wealth, which means that women have few exit strategies from unhappy or even life-threatening unions; the social acceptance of rape and violence against women; social proscriptions on travel; limitations on access to productive resources such as credit, technical and extension services and land. Women's lower political participation also gives them less opportunity to pressure decisionmakers to remove these inequalities.

[4] "Our goal must be to reduce these disparities across and within countries, to bring more and more people into the economic mainstream, to promote equitable access to the benefits of development regardless of nationality, race, or gender. This—the challenge of inclusion—is the key development challenge of our time." James D. Wolfensohn, at the World Bank Annual Meetings in Hong Kong, China, September 1997.

[5] See World Bank 2000f, Chapter 5.

SOCIAL RISK MANAGEMENT AND THE WORLD BANK'S WORK ON POVERTY REDUCTION

"The position of the rural population is like that of a man standing permanently up to his neck in water, so that even a ripple is sufficient to drown him."
— Ancient Chinese Proverb

The new framework of social risk management outlined in Chapter 2 has many intellectually attractive and operationally intuitive features. However, its true value depends on whether or not it succeeds in supporting improved policy advice, program design, and implementation capacity in countries. Here the full test is still incomplete, but early applications in preparing the World Bank's regional and country strategy papers[1] and rethinking several key aspects of the Bank's work in the social protection sector[2] have been very encouraging. This chapter and subsequent chapters will highlight some of the strategic conclusions of these applications (indicated by text in italics, preceded by an arrow, →).

An equally important test for the new framework relates to its usefulness and position within the World Bank's overarching mission of poverty reduction. At first glance, the traditional concept of poverty (insufficient income or consumption and lack of access to basic social services) and the main objective of social risk management (helping individuals, households, and communities to manage risks better) seem barely related. Yet the renewed worldwide focus on poverty has broadened the view of poverty and its main causes, fostered a more comprehensive view of the development process, and highlighted the need to address poverty in a more systematic manner. The new framework plays an important role in all the main initiatives on the development agenda—the *World Development Report*, the Comprehensive Development Framework, Poverty Reduction Strategy Papers, Social Principles, and Community-Driven Development—as described in more detail below.

SOCIAL RISK MANAGEMENT IN THE WORLD DEVELOPMENT REPORT

The World Development Report (WDR) 2000/1 updates the poverty focus of the 1980 and 1990 *WDRs* and, like the earlier reports, proposes a strategy for reducing poverty based on recent development experience and prospects for the coming decades. The report accepts the now traditional concept of poverty in terms of income/ consumption, education, health, and nutrition. It also extends the definition to include risk, vulnerability, powerlessness, and an inability to make oneself heard. The *WDR 2000/1* stresses the multidimensional character of poverty as a result of complex interactions among assets, markets, and institutions. It proposes to tackle poverty on three fronts by:

■ Increasing the capabilities of poor people and creating opportunities for them through complementary actions to stimulate overall growth, make markets work for them, and build their assets, including addressing deep-seated inequalities in the distribution of endowments such as education.

- Empowering poor people by giving them a voice and a chance to participate in the decisions that affect them.
- Providing security for poor people and reducing their vulnerability to the adverse effects of shocks by preventing the shocks from happening, by reducing the severity of their impact, and/or by helping them to cope.

The new *WDR* builds on the recent conceptual work around social risk management (Holzmann and Jorgensen 1999, 2000) and proposes that risk management and the broad range of social protection instruments should be at the core of the World Bank's work on poverty reduction. The conceptual framework of the report stresses different types of assets—physical, human, and social (Siegel and Alwang 1999, Alwang and Siegel 2000). The low monetary returns, volatility, and possible destruction (through, for example, health catastrophes or natural disasters) of all of these assets make poor people more vulnerable and cause poverty at the individual level. Hence, addressing these risks is critical to reducing poverty, and the *WDR 2000/1* deepens the analysis presented in Chapter 2 on the links between poverty, risk, and vulnerability.[3]

→ *As part of implementing the* WDR *findings, the World Bank's social protection sector will pay special attention to: (a) highlighting the importance of risk management in poverty reduction; (b) improving the measurement of risk and vulnerability; and (c) operationalizing the recommendations of the "security" section of the* WDR *report.*

RISK MANAGEMENT AND THE COMPREHENSIVE DEVELOPMENT FRAMEWORK

The Comprehensive Development Framework launched by World Bank President James Wolfensohn in 1998 takes a holistic view of development and poverty reduction by recommending that countries view development as a process of societal transformation and, thus, consider how all sectors can contribute to reducing poverty (Wolfensohn 1999). Identifying and putting appropriate policy actions in place in every sector requires governments to collaborate with other national and international actors such as nongovernmental organizations, trade unions, development banks, and United Nations organizations, as governmental actions alone will be insufficient.

The Comprehensive Development Framework analysis occurs at two levels: across an entire economy according to the links between poverty reduction and a population's opportunities, empowerment, and security; and by sector in terms of each actor's contribution. The social risk management matrix presented in Chapter 2 closely mirrors this second level of analysis by recognizing the importance of multiple actors.

→ *Social protection can play a role in terms of both analysis and action in the Comprehensive Development Framework: (a) in terms of the cross-sectoral linkages between security and poverty reduction (social protection as a theme), and (b) in terms of specific social protection interventions and the interplay between actors and instruments (social protection as a sector).*[4]

BOX 3.1

EXPENDITURE CHOICES AND SOCIAL RISK MANAGEMENT IN THE POOREST COUNTRIES

Analysis of direct public social protection spending (in its broadest sense) will be critical to strategic choices in the Heavily Indebted Poor Countries (HIPC) initiative. For example, there is little systematic analysis of the scale of public resources spent on various forms of social insurance and safety nets in Africa. These include drought relief, nutrition programs, subsidies on fertilizer and microcredit, social pensions, burial assistance, social assistance, and food-for-work schemes. All these programs are regarded as reducing the vulnerability of poor people (regardless of whether or not their incidence is pro-poor). Some fiscal and financial analysis of formal pension systems has been initiated in Africa, and individual countries are trying to take stock of the scale of their public safety nets (for example, Malawi and Zimbabwe). Yet, for the most part, countries have undertaken substantial outlays for transfers but do not have long-term strategies to guide or prioritize such spending. Future public expenditure analysis should consider expenditure incidence of the whole array of subsidies and transfer programs and should form part of the core HIPC work program.

Source: "Dynamic Risk Management and the Poor: Developing a Social Protection Strategy for Africa," World Bank 2000.

SOCIAL RISK MANAGEMENT AND POVERTY REDUCTION STRATEGY PAPERS

Poverty Reduction Strategy Papers (PRSPs) operationalize the Comprehensive Development Framework in a way that systematically links diagnosis and public actions to outcomes in specific country contexts. At the 1999 World Bank/IMF Annual Meetings, member states decided that debt relief in particular (under the enhanced Heavily Indebted Poor Countries initiative, HIPC) and concessional assistance in general (through the Poverty Reduction and Growth Facility and the International Development Association [IDA]) should be linked to the preparation of poverty reduction strategies by client countries.[5] The framework's focus on poverty outcomes and the link between policies and outcomes (see Box 3.1) underpin the multi-actor character of the Poverty Reduction Strategy approach and should ensure that debt relief is an integral part of poverty reduction efforts.

In developing their strategy papers, client countries have access to sourcebooks for various sectors prepared by the World Bank. The Social Protection sourcebook focuses on the analysis and instruments needed to help poor people handle key risks. The social risk management framework should also help the World Bank assess how effectively countries are providing risk management support by looking at their record on reducing vulnerability. The outcome indicators included in the sourcebook target risk and vulnerability, and the intermediate indicators should capture their determinants.

➔ *The integration of social risk management into the Poverty Reduction Strategy Papers calls for: (a) analysis of links between risks and poverty in a gender and country context; (b) review of country programs to support risk management; and (c) development of explicit recommendations for social protection interventions based on international good practice and country experience.*

SOCIAL RISK MANAGEMENT AND SOCIAL PRINCIPLES

Prompted by the East Asia crisis and the need to address its urgent social dimension, the World Bank/IMF Development Committee asked the World Bank to develop (in consultation with other institutions) "general principles of good practice" in social policies. These principles, presented at the Committee's spring meeting in 1999, called for a two-track approach in which the United Nations takes the lead role, with active support from the World Bank, in further developing the principles of social policy as part of the international community's commitment to follow up on the Copenhagen Declaration, and the World Bank, in collaboration with other partners, continues to distill lessons of good practice in implementing these principles and to help its member countries draw upon them in the pursuit of their economic and social development goals (World Bank 1999b).

This sector strategy paper reinforces the World Bank's work in this area and supports the ten commitments of the Copenhagen Declaration (see Box 1.1) and the follow-up Social Summit known as Geneva 2000. At Geneva, the world community committed itself to a goal of halving poverty rates by 2015. To meet this goal, concerted interventions are needed on all three aspects of poverty reduction (opportunity, empowerment, and security). The social risk management approach and the objectives of social protection are in line with all the specific commitments made in Copenhagen. They are particularly linked to the goals of poverty eradication (Commitment 2), the promotion of full employment and sustainable livelihoods (Commitment 3), and social integration (Commitment 4). Panels run in parallel with the Geneva 2000 summit discussed the social risk management approach and recognized its support of the Copenhagen goals. The PRSP Social Protection sourcebook and the Pension Reform Primer series already reflect the identification of best practice, while the "Asia Pacific Economic Cooperation (APEC) Social Safety Net Initiative" is currently extending the best practice approach (Chapter 2).

➔ *The World Bank will continue to integrate the social risk management approach in its ongoing work with United Nations institutions to develop principles of social policy, and will strengthen its work on distilling good practice, thus placing social protection and social risk management high on the global agenda.*

21

COMMUNITY-DRIVEN DEVELOPMENT

"What is it that the poor reply when asked what might make the greatest difference to their lives? They say, organizations of their own so that they may negotiate with government, with traders, and with NGOs. Direct assistance through community driven programs so they may shape their own destinies. Local ownership of funds, so that they may put a stop to corruption. They want NGOs and governments to be accountable to them."

James D. Wolfensohn, World Bank Annual Meetings, Fall 1999

SOCIAL RISK MANAGEMENT AND COMMUNITY-DRIVEN DEVELOPMENT

Community-driven development is a key strategy for implementing the Comprehensive Development Framework (CDF). By community-driven development, the World Bank refers to a process that "gives community organizations authority and control over decisions and resources" (World Bank 2000a). This includes direct responsibility for managing internal resources and external matching grants and making resource allocation decisions. It defines a process by which community groups organize and take action to achieve their common goals in the context of an enabling policy environment, and with support from responsive institutions (for example, private suppliers, local government, and national agencies).

One key indicator of community-driven development is the extent to which "communities manage internal and external funds themselves" (World Bank 2000a). The link between this definition and social risk management is clear. Social risk management is based on the notion that poor and vulnerable people manage risk and that governments and markets cannot do everything for them. Conversely, while communities and families can do much on their own (Box 3.2), they need support (from government, for example) to provide access to markets and public services.

The social protection sector of the World Bank has played a key role in developing a framework for community-driven development, and several of its key principles are already being implemented in a number of social funds (see Chapter 2, Guiding Principles; Chapter 5).

→ *The social protection sector will continue to play a leadership role in the conceptual and practical work necessary as the World Bank implements the strategy of community-driven development.*

NOTES FROM CHAPTER THREE

[1] See the regional Social Protection Sector Strategies summarized in Annex D. At the country level, Argentina, Benin, the Dominican Republic, Jamaica, Morocco, Nigeria, Pakistan, Togo, and Zimbabwe have used the framework to conceptualize social policy issues, and Colombia, Guatemala, Mexico, Nicaragua, and Peru plan to apply it in fiscal year 2001.

[2] The areas covered include social funds (Jorgensen and Van Domelen 2000), income support schemes for the unemployed (Vodopivec 2000), and the challenges and opportunities for provision of old-age security in East Asia (Holzmann, Mac Arthur, and Sin 2000).

[3] A recent comprehensive regional study also used a similar approach in its analysis (see de Ferranti and others 2000).

[4] Morocco is currently piloting the incorporation of social risk management into its Comprehensive Development Fund, and more country pilots are envisaged to gain firsthand experience.

[5] See IMF/IDA 1999; World Bank 1999a; World Bank 2000e.

PUTTING SOCIAL RISK MANAGEMENT TO WORK
BEYOND THE SOCIAL PROTECTION SECTOR

The social risk management framework has applications beyond the social protection sector, establishing social protection as a thematic issue (such as gender) in other sectors. Social risk management considerations apply to many aspects of the World Bank's work, including national shocks, financial reform, microfinance, rural development, the informal sector, infrastructure investments, health, population, nutrition, education, and gender issues. If appropriate policies are in place in these areas, then households are much less vulnerable. This indicates a need to build greater awareness of the importance of risk reduction for development. Furthermore, social risk management can be used as an analytical tool to assess interventions in various sectors. This chapter provides examples of the information sharing and analytical role that social risk management can and should play in selected areas beyond the traditional domain of social protection.

NATIONAL SHOCKS

Economic crises, natural disasters, and civil conflicts are the three most important causes of aggregate shocks to society, and each leads to sharp increases in the incidence of poverty (World Bank 2000f). Between 1990 and 1997, more than 80 percent of all developing countries experienced at least one year of negative per capita output growth as a result of these phenomena. Given these circumstances, the following observations and recommendations can be made:

■ Since many aggregate shocks are manmade, following from inappropriate macroeconomic policy or political conflict, there is a clear need for the World Bank to make governments aware of their negative effects on economic development in general, and on poor people in particular, and to encourage governments to adopt preventive policies.

■ Truly exogenous shocks such as natural disasters also lend themselves to preventive policies, such as the construction of earthquake-proof housing or dams, or the relocation of people—often poor people—to areas less likely to be affected. While costly (and often beyond the capacity of poor countries), these measures may prove to be cost-effective from a long-term present value consideration. This raises issues relating to financing (for example, present value trade-offs,

intertemporal government budget constraint, and the availability of short-term financing) and operational collaboration across sectors regarding physical and policy-related risks.

→ *The World Bank will work toward strengthening coordination in its support for interventions in disaster management and social protection.*

■ The covariant nature of aggregate shocks means that informal or market-based risk management instruments are often ineffective. However, this is not always the case. For example, insurance against natural risks can still function if appropriately structured and priced, and international diversification of assets and fiscal stabilization funds can smooth national consumption in an effective manner. The use of international insurance against natural risks is not yet well developed, but it should be encouraged since it has the potential to benefit poor people.

→ *The World Bank will encourage development and piloting of appropriate insurance products using the risk management framework.*

THE FINANCIAL SECTOR

The World Bank has been heavily involved in financial reform for many years, with a dramatic increase in lending during the recent global financial crisis. The reforms have mainly focused on building a strong, viable, formal financial sector in client countries.

A well-established financial sector is of fundamental importance in helping both the economy and individuals, both rich and poor, to handle risks. Almost by definition, financial markets exist to supply and price risk management instruments according to demand. Safe money and deposits are elementary but key risk management instruments, since they allow individuals to insure themselves by pooling their assets over time. Their existence enables individuals and households to cope with many idiosyncratic shocks, thereby representing a first line of effective defense, particularly for poor people.[1] Having multiple financial assets in portfolio with other assets (physical and social capital) constitutes a further level of risk management that allows the pooling of risk not only over time but also over other imperfectly correlated assets. Purchasing formal insurance is the optimal method of managing risk in a world of full information and perfect markets. But insurance markets are generally not inclusive due to asymmetric information and lack of appropriate risk pooling.

In most countries, a lack of access to market-based institutions, rather than inability to pay, prevents poor people from using savings as a form of risk management. In many areas, socially excluded groups are barred from using these institutions even if they have the financial means to do so. Instead of simply accepting this status quo, the public sector and donors could increase the access of poor people to safe financial services and assets in the following ways:

- Protect the financial assets of poor people by keeping inflation low, ensuring sound regulation and supervision, and promoting informal savings mechanisms and formal savings institutions.[2] Practical implementation information is available (for example, from the World Bank's Consultative Group to Assist the Poorest), but it needs to be reassessed in terms of its implications for risk mitigation and coping. Many of the microcredit programs that have successfully reached women, such as the Grameen Bank in Bangladesh and the Self-Employed Working Women's Association in India, now offer health and other kinds of insurance to women.

- Work with community-based groups and nongovernmental organizations to increase financial literacy, and include information and education campaigns to this end in financial sector instruments.
- Build links between poor entrepreneurs and the formal banking sector to break down the myths surrounding "the vulnerable as unsuitable customers" as, for example, the Chile Social Fund has done in linking small entrepreneurs with formal financial institutions.
- Support the creation of secondary insurance markets to give the formal sector an incentive to reach out to poor and excluded segments of the population with insurance and banking products.

→ *In supporting macroeconomic and financial sector reforms, the World Bank will pay increased attention to the needs of poor people for appropriate financial instruments to help them manage risk.*

RURAL DEVELOPMENT AND EXTENDING THE RISK POOL

The lack of alternative risk management instruments often forces poor rural households to adopt self-insurance strategies that are disadvantageous in terms of direct and opportunity costs. This hinders them from efficiently managing their limited portfolio of assets and from adopting more productive technologies, which, in turn, results in more risks, decreased returns, and perpetuation of the vicious cycle of poverty.

The World Bank is considering several innovative ways to manage rural risk, notably manifestations of commodity price and yield fluctuations at the macro (national), meso (community and local government), and micro (household) levels (see Siegel and Alwang 1999).[3] These include: (a) commodity price management using international and domestic commodity and finance/insurance markets; (b) disaster management with a focus on risk reduction and mitigation using various technological approaches (for example, advance warning systems) and finance or insurance instruments; (c) rural finance (notably microfinance) with credit and savings for agricultural and nonagricultural production and consumption, along with some insurance instruments and new types of interlinked contracts; (d) crop insurance programs that have objective criteria for collecting damage payments and that cover both those with and without land, agricultural and nonagricultural sectors in rural areas, and urban areas; (e) safety nets based on self-targeting of employment and food programs that are universally accessible at all times; and (f) various community-based programs financed by social funds (Jorgensen and Van Domelen 2000).

→ *The World Bank will strengthen the linkages in its support for rural development and social protection, including the development and monitoring of pilot programs.*

INFRASTRUCTURE INVESTMENTS

Infrastructure investments such as the construction of a road, an irrigation system, or a dam have an important bearing on the development of an economy and on the opportunities available to poor people. In the past, the central and often only criterion used to evaluate such investments has been the estimated rate of return.

In addition to economic effects, these investments also have an important impact on the vulnerability of individuals. These effects may not be equally distributed, thereby possibly decreasing vulnerability for some and increasing it for others, at least in the short run (for example, through resettlement). The construction of a road between an isolated village and a market town reduces the vulnerability of the village community by making it easier for people to trade their goods, migrate, and access financial market institutions and their instruments. Similarly, irrigation projects are useful in reducing output risk in agriculture when rainfall is unpredictable. The construction of a dam can be the key instrument for preventing flooding in agricultural and residential areas. These risk reduction or mitigation effects of infrastructure are often not taken into account in assessing the costs and benefits of a potential investment, and as yet the data and analytical toolkits needed to assess vulnerability effects do not exist.

→ *Where appropriate, data should be gathered on the risk prevention aspects of infrastructure investments and toolkits should be prepared to ensure that vulnerability effects are taken into account in infrastructure project planning.*

HEALTH, NUTRITION, POPULATION, AND EDUCATION

This section briefly outlines how the social risk management framework applies to the health, nutrition, population, and education sectors, as well as to borderline areas that cut across human development. Like the social protection sector in the past, the human development sectors have all too often adopted a sectoral approach, which has made it harder to coordinate interventions in areas of potential synergy.[4] While the primary role of the human development sectors is to build human capital, adopting a holistic social risk management approach can help achieve this.

In health, preventive and other basic health services (for example, immunizations) are generally very important risk reduction measures. The existence of a good health care system increases the ability of poor people to mitigate the impact of a potential health shock, and the curative side is important to help poor people cope once the shock has occurred (see Box 4.1).

In the area of health insurance, social risk management relates most closely to risk mitigation and risk coping. The focus of health insurance for poor people needs to be on catastrophic illness. Compulsory participation, the introduction of waiting periods, and household or community collective insurance could reduce adverse

---

BOX 4.1

THE DISASTROUS EFFECTS OF A HEALTH SHOCK IN LAO CAI PROVINCE, VIETNAM

Nha is 26 years old and his family has twelve members. The family used to be one of the richest in the village, but is now one of the poorest. It has suffered two shocks in recent years. First, Nha's father died two years ago, so there are now only two main laborers in the family—Nha and his mother, who is 40 years old. Nha has two young children. Two years ago, his daughter Lu Seo Pao had a serious illness and had to undergo operations in the district and province hospitals. Nha's family had to sell four buffaloes, one horse, and two pigs to cover the expenses of treatment. The operation cost several million Vietnamese Dong, but the child is still not cured. All the people in his community helped, but no one could offer more than 20,000 Vietnamese Dong. Moreover, Nha's younger brother—Lu Seo Seng, who was in grade 6—had to leave school in order to help his family. Nha says that, if Lu Seo Pao had not become ill, his family would still have many buffaloes, he would have a house for his younger brother to live in, and Seng could have continued his studies.

Source: World Bank, 1999c.

selection and increase risk pooling and sustainability. Poor families may not always be able to afford to put aside resources for a health-specific insurance fund. One possible alternative is a general savings account with withdrawal restricted to times of catastrophic or major expenditure needs. They can be multipurpose (not just for medical emergencies), so that poor people would be more willing to save, and can be protected by strict enforcement of the "catastrophic event" withdrawal rule. This type of savings/insurance mechanism could be developed on a pilot basis by informal financial institutions or non-governmental organizations.

The role of traditional health practitioners and indigenous medicine has not received sufficient attention in health sector reform programs. Most poor people in Africa use traditional healers and indigenous medicinal plants as their first line of defense against health shocks. Community support is needed to identify the safest and most efficacious of these plants and other environmental resources and practices, increase their availability, and promote greater synergies between the Western and traditional medicinal systems. Health policies in South Africa, Ghana, and Ethiopia are starting to move in the direction of better integration. This approach needs to be pursued in more countries as a potentially cost-effective means of reducing the exposure of poor people to chronic and acute health risks.

Nutrition risk management measures are crucial for prevention (household food security and good weaning and feeding practices), mitigation (storing food in case of an income crisis), and coping (food transfers and food for work). Many of the small yet frequent income losses of poor people in Africa due to illnesses are linked to malnutrition, the lack of a safe water supply, and poor sanitation. Greater and more integrated investments in these areas may be a more cost-effective tool for reducing this type of noncatastrophic risk than health insurance schemes.

Some *population* issues relate to risk management (such as the practice of having large families as a form of insurance or diversifying assets) and risk reduction (the link between lower fertility and lower health risks, for example).

In the *education* sector, the social risk management framework can provide new understanding in several ways:

■ The best risk reducer is an excellent formal education. Too often, vocational education and training are used to try to fix the problems left over by an inadequate education system; this is inefficient and inequitable.

■ Service providers often introduce user fees in education (and health) with the assumption that public safety nets will take care of the poorest people. Yet this is often not a realistic assumption, especially in poorer countries with lower levels of institutional development.

■ After a covariant shock, a good option may be to introduce safety net programs that can support the continued demand for education by poor people (for example, school fee exemptions and grants associated with continued school attendance). In the absence of such transfer mechanisms directly linked to social sector service use, short-term shocks can permanently damage the human development outcomes of poor people. There is evidence (for example, from Indonesia in the aftermath of the financial crisis) that poor people reduce their consumption of education services as a risk-coping mechanism, which almost always causes irreversible income losses in poor households. This type of program should be a priority in countries that have relatively high administrative capacity in the public or private sectors.

Finally, the social risk management perspective is important to a number of areas that cut across the human development sectors:

■ Preventing disability is mainly a matter of preventive health measures and occupational safety (plus conflict prevention). Its mitigation involves providing inclusive education and appropriate insurance, and coping requires curative health care and safety nets.

■ Early childhood development services—targeting the most rapid period of human development—provide an exceptional opportunity to reduce risks and improve human capital in general. Since early childhood development programs tend to generate fiscal savings by lowering school repetition rates and/or social welfare transfers, they are also fiscally affordable in low-income countries.

■ In its policies on the elderly, the World Bank's focus has tended to be on pensions. However, the social risk management framework should lead the World Bank to direct more attention to a wider array of human development concerns relating to the elderly, additional means of income support, and lifelong learning. These issues become especially important in view of the dramatic demographic transition to an older population that is occurring in many parts of the developing world.

■ It is now almost a cliché to advocate tackling the HIV/AIDS epidemic through a multisectoral approach rather than strictly through the health care system. The multisectoral approach requires more active cooperation among various groups, including National Multisector AIDS Committees, district or community groups, Joint United Nations Program on HIV/AIDS (UNAIDS), governments at all levels, donors, employers, and social funds. It is important to identify and distinguish between delivery mechanisms that are most effective for prevention, care, and coping. Analytical work on social risk management and AIDS (begun with UNAIDS) and operational work on how social protection instruments could better support AIDS management will be necessary. The latter area is especially relevant for social funds. The gender dimensions of HIV/AIDS also merit more attention. In many cultures the burden of caring for victims, which may entail sacrificing employment and education opportunities, falls almost exclusively on women. Women are also more frequently ostracized when they become victims of AIDS and may even be forced to leave their communities.

Developing such integrated approaches to human development is most important in poorer, less institutionally developed countries. In a Sub-Saharan African country, for instance, it may be better to manage risks by strengthening basic health and education services, early childhood development, and AIDS prevention before taking more traditional social protection measures. On the coping side, however, there is still a need for a mix of social protection and other human development-related interventions.

→ *To address these cross-cutting human development issues, the World Bank is developing an operational strategy that builds on the existing sectoral strategies in health, nutrition, population, education, and social protection. A human capital development framework with a social risk management focus will be the cornerstone of such a strategy.*

SOCIAL RISK MANAGEMENT AND GENDER

Analysis of social risk management and actions to lower vulnerability must take gender differences into account. Although women and men share many of the burdens of poverty, vulnerability, and risk, socially imposed constraints in most societies also place women in an inferior situation. Women and men are often able to manage risk in different ways. For instance, women frequently have less education and thus are less able to reduce many risks (such as underemployment and disease). In addition, restrictions on women's ownership of assets and the low quality of their property rights (for example, land tenure) may decrease women's ability to mitigate risk. Even though they carry the main burden of coping with shocks to the family, such as illness or droughts, laws or norms may restrict their access to services that could help them cope better (for example, curative health services).

Social gender disparities are not only inequitable but also lead to economically inefficient outcomes, resulting in reduced ability to manage risk. The Policy Research Report entitled "Engendering Development" (World Bank 2000b) argues that gender inequality is costly to

---

BOX 4.2

27

GENDER INEQUALITY AND POVERTY REDUCTION

Evidence is growing that gender disparities are not only inequitable but also lead to economically inefficient outcomes, including reduced ability to manage risk. Evidence from many countries shows that disparities between women's and men's access to, and control over, resources relates to systematically lower access to health and education facilities among women, which leads to less than optimal levels of participation in economic activities (Elson 1991; Anker 1998). Macro-level studies also confirm that better-educated women contribute to the welfare of the next generation by reducing infant and child mortality, lowering fertility, and improving the nutritional status of children (Hill and King 1995; Klasen 1999; Smith and Haddad 2000). Additional evidence points to the significant negative impact of gender inequality in secondary education on economic growth: a one percent increase in the share of women in secondary school education is associated with a 0.3 percent increase in per capita income (Dollar and Gatti 1999).

development and provides extensive support for this assertion. Rigid gender roles are often barriers to risk management, just as they are to static poverty reduction (Box 4.2). There is no doubt that the contribution of women to household income and production is crucial for reducing poverty. Many families rely on women's production to keep them out of poverty or to keep them from falling even deeper into poverty. Therefore, it is critical to address men and women differently, rather than thinking of poor and vulnerable people as an undifferentiated group.

→ *In its work on poverty reduction, the World Bank will take account of gender-based differences in social risk management, especially regarding limitations on women's ability to accomplish it.*

NOTES FROM CHAPTER FOUR

[1] As seen earlier, the alternative for poor people is disinvestment in human capital, which endangers future development prospects.

[2] These include postal banks, which have a broad network and low transaction costs for small savers.

[3] Many of these finance, insurance, safety net, community-based programs, and technical strategies are really new attempts at old approaches. However, the new programs take account of the lessons learned over the years and changed conditions in developing countries.

[4] The human development sectors recognize this and will further develop an integrated approach in the coming years.

28

PUTTING SOCIAL RISK MANAGEMENT TO WORK
IN THE SOCIAL PROTECTION SECTOR

While Chapter 4 examined social risk management across a number of sectors and themes, this chapter applies the framework to the social protection sector. This process involves rethinking public sector programs against the benchmark of social risk management and expanding the notion of social protection to explicitly include support for market-based and informal risk management activities—areas in which the World Bank has some experience on which the sector can build.

STRENGTHENING PUBLIC SOCIAL PROTECTION INTERVENTIONS

Distinctions among risk reduction, mitigation, and coping strategies are important in this analysis. Most of the sector's labor market interventions[1] fall into the category of public support for risk reduction (see Table 2.2), with the exception of income support for the unemployed, which is a risk mitigation effort. Most social insurance programs relate to mitigation,[2] even though some of the basic income support for the elderly and sick overlaps with coping. Safety nets fit squarely into the coping category, even though the social risk management framework indicates that safety nets should not only help people cope in the short run but also support longer-run risk reduction or mitigation. This section maintains the reduction/mitigation/coping distinction while discussing various public interventions, even though many programs involve more than one strategy. At the end, the section highlights how improved information and communication technology can support social risk management efforts.

Reducing Risk

Reducing the probability of downside risk is a powerful instrument of social risk management. Many risk reduction efforts remain outside the scope of social protection, such as maintaining macroeconomic stability, creating sound financial markets, adopting growth-oriented policies, and establishing preventive measures against natural disasters (Chapter 4). Some social protection instruments that support risk reduction are, however, essentially linked to the labor market.[3]

Providing Equitable and Inclusive Labor Markets. Since labor is often poor people's main or only asset, equitable access to safe and well-paid employment is one of the most important aspects of risk reduction. Formalization of the labor relationship is reflected in basic standards, including the prohibition of forced labor and discrimination in employment and pay, the freedom of association, and the right to collective bargaining. Since the last two standards have political as well as economic implications, some countries are reluctant to embrace them. Furthermore, the empirical evidence about their economic benefits is mixed. The World Bank will continue to review the empirical analyses. The available evidence suggests that good industrial relations between employers and employees may keep an economy stable and, with responsible leadership, may prevent settlements that are detrimental to outsiders, who are often poor. The evidence further indicates that to achieve this potential win-win outcome, core labor standards must go hand in hand with building institutional capacity and trust between the market partners and the government.

A promising complement to public labor standards is private or market-based standards established by stakeholders (such as consumers, employers, workers, and nongovernmental organizations). These standards range from corporate benchmarking, codes of conduct, and voluntary enforcement of industry standards, to consumer activism in favor of labeling (Sabel, O'Rouke, and Fung 2000). More knowledge about private standards—their potential and limits—and the interplay between public and private standards would help to make labor markets more equitable and inclusive,

THE IFC AND LABOR PROTECTION

The IFC is exploring appropriate best practice goals and ways to work with its clients to achieve a significant development impact on both workers and communities. Following the March 1998 adoption of a *Harmful Child and Forced Labor Policy*, IFC has been pursuing other labor protection related tasks:

- *Preparation of a harmful child labor guide.* The guide will assist clients in eliminating harmful child labor in their own and their value chain operations. The guide has been prepared based on extensive consultation with IFC clients worldwide and with other industries and business associations, NGOs, and government agencies.
- *Preparation of a labor practices discussion paper.* The paper assesses the global experience in implementation and overall development impact of core labor standards, and considers the implications of these practices on IFC's development mission.
- *Preparation of a retrenchment guide.* IFC support for the privatization of state enterprises often involves downsizing of the labor force and can cause severe economic and social problems. The loss of income sources and related benefits, such as access to health care and education, can cause long-term hardship and impoverishment unless appropriate compensation and mitigation measures are carefully planned and implemented. This document will provide guidance on how to deal with these issues in a practical and flexible manner with due consideration of local conditions and requirements.
- *Updating of health and safety guidelines.* The WHO has estimated that chronic illness associated with working conditions, preventable injuries, and deaths in high-risk working environments cause approximately 3 percent of the global burden of disease. Sanctions available to national agencies and inspectorates to protect workers' health and safety are generally far less compelling than corporate standards and regulation in the workplace. IFC has existing guidelines on Health and Safety, which are currently being updated.
- *Completion of a Community Development Resource Guide.* The guide, accompanied by case studies, is intended as a resource to support IFC clients and other companies' efforts to establish effective community development programs. These programs promote sustainable economic growth and support livelihoods, education, skills building, and the health and welfare of a company's stakeholders, particularly people who are located near or affected by a company's operations.

thereby contributing to risk reduction. Pilot programs in the area of private standards will be undertaken in close cooperation with International Finance Corporation (IFC) (Box 5.1).

Other priority labor standards involve minimum wage regulations, a minimum working age, job safety and security provisions (including for women), and severance pay. These regulations, while protecting workers, also increase labor market rigidities. More research will be necessary to understand the most effective ways to increase labor mobility and generate employment while protecting workers from harmful situations.

→ *The World Bank Group will approach issues surrounding public labor market standards on a pragmatic and country-by-country basis. The Bank will learn from the experience of the International Labor Organization (ILO) and other international organizations and will work with the private sector and the ILO on complementary private standards on a pilot basis.*

Enhancing Pre- and In-Service Skills. A special challenge for any country is to build a system for helping the workforce develop new and better skills. Continuous skill enhancement is crucial in a world economy in which human capital development increasingly drives growth. Equally important is the distribution of such growth among the population, since low-skilled workers are much more likely to become unemployed, stay unemployed for longer, and become increasingly marginalized. Pre- and in-service skill training is closely dependent on the quality of the education system but is also influenced by the structure of the labor market, the wage-setting process, and the incentives and opportunities that workers have to enhance their skills.

Experience with government-run training programs has been rather mixed. As a result, these programs have changed over time from being driven by the needs of the public sector to being driven by demand from the labor market. While the role of the government as a provider of programs is becoming limited, its role as a (co-)sponsor, incentive setter, or quality insurer is likely to continue to be important. While there is no blueprint for skills enhancement, countries at different stages of development provide important lessons (Gill, Fluitman, and Dar 2000) that should help to develop a new poverty reduction and development-oriented paradigm.

→ *The World Bank Group will work with national and international partners (including the private sector through the IFC) to pilot new approaches to skills-training projects through lending and to rework existing projects through the sector's quality enhancement program.*

Eliminating Harmful Child Labor. Currently, an estimated 250 million children are working worldwide. In its most abusive form, child labor prevents children from receiving education, exposes them to damaging health risks, and limits their physical and mental development. Each of these effects will have a negative impact on their future earnings, thereby risking the perpetuation of poverty in the next generation. Thus, reducing or eliminating harmful child labor is a powerful tool to dampen the risks of poverty in adulthood for many children today.

Until now, the World Bank has addressed child labor by working to increase access to and relevance of education. Recently, however, with support from the government of Norway, the Bank has followed the lead of UNICEF and the ILO in taking direct actions to reduce child labor. Measures currently being tested include providing parents, employers, and society as a whole with information on the long-term welfare losses associated with child labor, strengthening the position of children and women within families, and supporting targeted conditional transfer programs that make social assistance contingent upon family efforts to keep children in school and away from harmful labor (see Fallon and Tzannatos 1998).

→ *The complex nature and global scope of the child labor problem is likely to require the World Bank to follow the lead of ILO and UNICEF, shift from evaluations and analytical work to the implementation of more pilot projects, and cooperate more closely with the private sector.*

Disability. People with disabilities are an underserved group in most developing countries. Estimates for developing countries are poor, but disability may affect up to 10 percent of the world's population. Although the connection is not well documented, disability in the household can lead to poverty because it is often associated with exclusion from school or the workplace, as well as stress due to intrafamily dependence.

Many sectors of the World Bank are developing and extending their products and services to help clients confront the disability issue. The challenge for the World Bank is to develop high-quality activities that are appropriate to the circumstances and means of its clients. Work must be done to identify the causes and consequences of disability, the best practices to reduce its occurrence/incidence, and ways to mitigate its effects.

→ *The World Bank's social protection sector will focus on ensuring that disability is taken into account in social protection interventions, such as pension reform and social fund operations.*

Mitigating Risk

Not all risks can or should be eliminated. The absence of (downside) risk is likely to reduce individual work efforts, and the prospect of (upside) risk is a crucial element for entrepreneurial activities and education decisions—the motor of economic growth. Insufficient risk mitigation can have negative welfare implications, forcing people into insufficient or irregular consumption patterns. Also, the absence of risk-mitigating instruments makes people (especially poor people) more risk-averse. Therefore, risk-mitigating instruments that maximize benefits while minimizing costs are needed, particularly in the areas of old-age income security and unemployment benefits.

Old-Age Income Security. The World Bank's proposal for a multipillar approach to pension reform (World Bank 1994) shaped the discussion and implementation of pension reform worldwide. The multipillar system consists of three "pillars": (a) a publicly managed, unfunded, defined benefit scheme; (b) a privately managed, fully funded, defined contribution plan; and (c) voluntary

31

retirement savings in the form of housing, insurance, or other assets. The first pillar should take care of poverty concerns, and the second should provide income replacement. This approach should create more equitable and affordable pensions and better safeguards against an aging population and political risk (for example, expropriation by powerful groups). It should also interfere less in individual labor supply and saving decisions, contribute to national savings and financial market development, help protect older people from poverty, and better handle increases in longevity (James 1998).

The World Bank has evolved into a key player and recognized depository of knowledge on pension reform,

working on pension issues in some 60 countries in the 1990s. Annex A presents in detail the worldwide experience with pension reform and the World Bank's involvement. While almost all World Bank-supported reforms have moved in the direction of a multipillar system, no two reforms have been identical. This reflects the differences among countries in terms of their starting conditions, economic and social environments, and national preferences. The absence of a rigid blueprint for pension reform means that the World Bank emphasizes the conditions that must be fulfilled to trigger its support, which include distributive objectives, financial sustainability, macroeconomic feasibility, a sound regulatory and supervisory framework, and sufficient administrative capacity (Holzmann 2000).

The experience in countries moving toward a multipillar pension system (with a large, privately managed, fully funded, and defined benefit pillar) has highlighted areas where multipillar pension schemes contribute to effective and efficient social risk management. The main areas needing further attention include coverage, gender (see Box 5.2), administrative costs, annuities, governance, and financial market regulation and supervision. The World Bank is now conducting important research and knowledge management on these topics.[4]

→ *The World Bank's future work on pension reform will focus more on the provision of retirement benefits for people in the informal sector and on old-age income support for the life-time poor through public noncontributory schemes and community support. This will be reflected in second-generation reform loans and the continuation and updating of the Pension Reform Primer series (see "Knowledge Management" in Chapter 6).*

Providing Appropriate Unemployment Benefits. Even with well-functioning labor markets, there are times when a person is underemployed or unemployed. Receiving unemployment benefits prevents workers from experiencing large consumption losses and, at the extreme, falling into poverty. There are also efficiency implications, since workers with the promise of income support are more likely to agree to accept temporary unemployment as a result of enterprise or sector restructuring. The traditional approach to mitigating this risk, widely used in OECD countries, has been unemployment insurance. However, this is probably inappropriate for most developing and transition countries, in which the shocks are more covariant, the informal sector is larger, and adminis-

---

| BOX 5.2 |

GENDER AND THE DESIGN OF OLD-AGE SECURITY

Specific design features of a formal pension system, such as the statutory retirement age and provisions for survivors' benefits or a minimum pension guarantee, all matter to the relative benefit flows that women and men receive. Reforms in many countries have sought to link benefits more closely to work histories, to encourage a long working life. While the new norms may appear to be gender neutral, work histories are often different for men and women, since women tend to have shorter work histories because of time out of the labor force to care for children. For example, in several countries of the former Soviet Union (Kazakhstan, the Kyrgyz Republic, Latvia, and Moldova), the new systems deliberately penalize early retirement and reward longer careers. With no change in behavior or policy, women's pensions will therefore generally be less than men's. (The implicit financial returns for women remain, on average, higher than for men due to women's longer life expectancy and redistributory minimum pensions.) The net change in wealth from the reforms is, however, higher on average for men than for women, because men work longer and get a higher pension. Women's longer life expectancy means that women can expect to spend the last years of their life alone. If their pensions are too low because of their work histories, the incidence of elderly poverty may increase.

Source: Castel and Fox 2001

trative capacity is low. Alternative instruments could include means-tested unemployment assistance, social assistance, public works programs, and severance pay from earmarked individual saving accounts (a still largely untested measure).

→ *World Bank work on unemployment benefits will focus on assessing which instruments are best for different country environments, including an evaluation of existing experiences, and piloting in countries where there is sufficient interest to do so, all in close cooperation with the ILO and interested regional development banks.*

Coping with Risk

To cope with a risk once it has occurred is the last and often only social risk management option. The government has an important role in ensuring rights to financial and real assets that can be drawn upon in a crisis, but for poor people who have no assets, the government is the provider of last resort.

There are three main forms of public risk-coping assistance: (a) needs-based cash transfers; (b) in-kind transfers, subsidies, and fee waivers; and (c) public works. Each has advantages and disadvantages and presents different options for dealing with issues such as targeting, coverage, and incentive effects. The appropriate size and mix of programs will vary from country to country. Moreover, with all of these programs it is important to understand the cultural factors determining resource allocation within the household. For example, targeting strategies must recognize that, in many cultures, women and girls receive proportionately less food and other consumption goods than their male counterparts.

Needs-Based Cash Transfers. In an ideal setting, the intention of targeted cash transfers is to bring every person up to a predefined minimum level of consumption. In the real world, however, many obstacles emerge. These include: (a) estimating and choosing the poverty line, (b) designing the system and administering means-tests, (c) establishing budgetary requirements, (d) finding the best way to make the transfers to the communities or households, and (e) devising incentive mechanisms for poor people, and (f) dealing with the symptoms and not the causes of poverty. Countries are using a variety of other instruments, including proxy targeting, food subsidies, food stamps, and categorical benefits (such as social pensions and family benefits) and are experimenting with alternative delivery

mechanisms, including outsourcing to the private sector and nongovernmental organizations.

In-Kind Transfers, Subsidies, and Fee Waivers. Subsidies for goods (for example, food and fuel) and services have been, and in some countries still are, the main means of providing income support for poor people in and after crises. However, empirical research indicates that, in general, they benefit the better-off more than the poor. Even when poor people do benefit, the income effect is typically small while the cost to the public budget is high. For this reason, most countries are now implementing subsidy reduction programs. Something is needed to replace these subsidies, but all of the possible alternatives have imperfections. In-kind transfers of food, for example, may have undesirable incentive effects and incur large administrative costs associated with transportation and distribution, although such transfers have added benefits in terms of making the goods directly available to beneficiaries.

A special form of selective subsidy involves waiving fees for school attendance or health care for poor people during an economic crisis. If the truly poor can be properly identified—for example, through screening by the local community—then effective targeting will be possible. Indonesia applied this approach with apparent success during the recent crisis (Sayed and Filmer 1998). If substantiated by other experiences, this could be one way to prevent poor people from coping with shocks by taking their children out of school or by forgoing necessary health care.

Public Works Programs. These programs, in which the unemployed or underemployed earn income from temporary jobs mainly in the provision, repair, and upgrading of infrastructure, offer a number of theoretical advantages. The work requirement is a self-targeting mechanism, especially if salaries are kept low (at or below the market rate for unskilled labor), meaning that only the needy will apply for the jobs. The programs create some infrastructure, which, if well targeted (for example, a road in a poor area), provides poor people with added benefits and a better ability to manage risks. These advantages, along with the operational experience in countries such as India (Maharashtra) and Argentina, have led to calls for more permanent public works programs (Box 5.3), given the difficulties of scaling up programs quickly, as experienced in Korea recently (Prescott 1999).

On the negative side, the cost of transferring benefits through public works programs is often high because of the need to finance materials and other inputs in addition to labor. In some countries, it has proven difficult to get to a labor intensity of more than 30 percent. This problem is compounded by an apparent trade-off between the degree of labor intensity and the quality of the infrastructure created. In addition, politicians often use these programs to help increase support for the governing party, and there have been serious allegations of corruption in many countries, mostly in programs where community involvement and project management have been absent or low. Yet the programs have so many potential benefits that it is important to attempt their improvement by thoroughly reviewing existing projects and involving communities in project selection and management.

In light of the social risk management approach, there is a need to focus on the following questions:

→ **How can the World Bank sustain its support for safety net design and implementation?**
The focus will be on impact assessment and lessons from different institutional designs, while being as responsive as possible in lending (especially in crisis situations). Important analytical work is currently ongoing with the IMF and the Asian and Inter-American Development Banks under the aegis of the Asia-Pacific Economic Cooperation process.

→ **What is the appropriate balance in supporting the three types of coping?**
Since each type of coping has drawbacks and advantages, information on program experience will be systematically collected and analyzed to provide the best advice possible to client countries. The World Bank is increasingly being asked for such advice, especially regarding which programs to scale up or down in a crisis situation.

→ **How much is enough?**
While the global financial crisis has emphasized the need for coping programs, care must be taken to ensure that they remain appropriately sized and do not hamper other forms of risk management. For example, if a country increases its debt to pay for transfers, its ability to invest in human and physical capital in the future may decline, thus reducing individuals' ability to manage risk. Such issues must enter the World Bank's dialogue with the IMF in crisis situations.

→ **How can coping assistance help with risk mitigation and reduction?**
From the perspective of the social risk management framework, this relates to how social assistance can be provided in a way that not only increases current levels of consumption for poor people, but also enables them

BOX 5.3

PERMANENT PUBLIC WORKS PROGRAMS

Establishing delivery mechanisms for coping instruments has proven difficult during crises, when support is needed most. This has led to calls for permanent work programs "simmering" during normal times, which are accessible to individuals without work, and which can be expanded once a crisis hits. The ideal project would involve:

- **Participatory selection of projects that provide a net value added (positive rate of return) and not only targeted income support;**
- **Work opportunities at below the prevailing market wage in a self-selecting and targeted manner;**
- **A trained administration that could scale up projects according to the gravity of the crisis; and**
- **A protected source of available funds, ideally internationally diversified.**

This safety net concept has great intellectual appeal. But its implementation faces all the challenges outlined in the text about public works in general, with the additional complications presented by the fact that it would have to be able to be "on stand-by." The Korea experience further demonstrates the difficulties in scaling up when a major crisis hits. In an ideal world, cash transfer programs would work the same way, but in reality they have never been scaled up successfully in a crisis. More promising avenues for developing a "simmering" safety net may involve the distribution of food to children falling below a given nutritional standard. Such a program would have clear benchmarks for scaling up or back, based on pre-established nutrition levels, which would offer indications regarding the necessary scale of the program as a whole.

Source: Based on Ravallion 1999

34

to better manage risk and climb out of poverty. Analytically, this would argue for providing assistance in the form of asset transfers, investment opportunities, and empowerment, especially for marginalized groups. Research and pilot programs are needed in this area.

Information and Communications Technology

Information and communications technology (ICT) is developing at a rapid pace. It is a critical factor in social and economic development, as well as for social risk management and social protection. Transferring technology, management skills, and know-how is crucial for three main reasons:

- Reducing the "digital divide." Given the short innovation cycles of ICT, the technological gap between industrial countries and the developing and transition countries is already wide and is likely to widen. Facilitating the transfer of technology and skills is the only way to prevent developing countries from falling farther behind in this aspect of development.

- Improving the business process. Applying ICT is not merely a case of automating existing administrative procedures. It involves restructuring current business processes in social protection systems, which are often extremely inefficient, leading to low contribution collection for social security programs (such as old age, disability, health, sickness, and unemployment), inadequate file keeping and client contacts, and delays in disbursement.

- Redesigning social protection programs. Good ICT systems require rethinking the design and delivery of social programs. For example, automated filing systems allow the identification of hardship cases as well as cross-checking among the beneficiaries of social programs. This permits a different design of social safety nets as well as the provision of (virtual) one-stop shops for all social programs. South Africa, for example, uses mobile cash payout machines that recognize fingerprints in the distribution of its social pension. This benefits up to 80 percent of the elderly population, which is mainly illiterate and lacks forms of identification typical of industrialized countries (Case and Deaton 1996).

Financing social protection projects containing ICT components would increase the efficiency and effectiveness of service delivery, thus making it easier for vulnerable people to manage risk.

→ *The World Bank will intensify its work with clients to incorporate appropriate information and communications technology into projects and to review its procurement processes to facilitate implementation.*

PUBLIC SUPPORT FOR INFORMAL AND MARKET-BASED INSTRUMENTS

As discussed in the previous chapters, the majority of poor people have only informal mechanisms of risk management. While prevalent, these mechanisms are neither inclusive of the poorest people nor very effective (and may even be detrimental), especially when the shocks are large and covariant. This means that the development community needs to find ways to support, or "crowd in," prodevelopment informal mechanisms to make them more effective and inclusive and discourage, or "crowd out," the detrimental ones.

Putting more emphasis on informal and community-based social protection services should not be seen as "giving up" on public structures. On the contrary, building up communities' ability to manage risk better enables them to start demanding better services from the public sector as well. To achieve functioning public sector services, actors at the lowest possible level (local government and the constituency they represent) must be strong and have a sense of mutual accountability.

The World Bank has some experience in improving the functioning of informal and market-based interventions, but it needs to learn more from what others are doing. This section discusses some of the World Bank's key products and strategic moves to meet the challenges identified in three selected areas of activity: (a) scaling up social funds to expand community-driven development; (b) supporting informal risk management by expanding legal reform and legal assistance and "new" safety net activities; and (c) increasing poor people's access to market-based interventions by giving a risk management perspective to financial reforms and re-emphasizing microfinance.

Scaling Up Social Funds to Expand Community-Driven Development

Social funds are agencies that finance small-scale projects based on demand from poor communities and other local groups. Communities provide some of the financing to ensure that the proposals are truly needed. Social funds appraise, finance, and supervise interventions, but it is the private sector or the communities themselves that implement them. In the social risk management framework, social funds have a demonstrated ability to involve many actors in risk management (including nongovernmental organizations, communities, the private sector, and governments) and to build on community-based interventions (informal risk management techniques) to improve the effectiveness of public sector interventions.

The Bolivian government established the first social fund in 1987. Now more than 50 countries have agencies that are either called social funds or share their characteristics. No two social funds are exactly the same. Their objectives include building social capital, providing services and infrastructure, and supporting decentralization and income generation. They are present in all regions, with the greatest concentration in Latin America and Sub-Saharan Africa. Eastern Europe and Central Asia have most recently incorporated the approach. As discussed in Chapter 2, social funds do well in terms of targeting and sustainable impact (also see Bigio 1998).

Social funds have a multifaceted and changing position in the social risk management matrix (Table 2.2). They started out in the lower right-hand corner of the matrix, in the form of support for public works programs. They have now moved both upwards and to the left, toward more community management of programs and emphasis on investments that lead to risk reduction (for example, in preventive health care, water supply, and basic education). In the future, these funds will likely play a larger role in risk reduction and encourage the development of informal risk management arrangements. Social funds will also have to give more attention to:

■ Fostering the flow and sustainability of benefits from the infrastructure they finance, and maximizing its impact (rather than just output);
■ Targeting on the basis of vulnerability as well as poverty by differentiating contribution levels, developing model projects for specific vulnerable groups, and putting these groups in contact with existing government programs;
■ Increasing the promotion of services in areas such as finance, legal assistance, preventive health projects, empowerment training, income generation, financial literacy, and pilot support for informal, community-based risk management; and,
■ Strengthening the focus on building social capital and local organizational capacity through better participatory techniques and decentralization of decisionmaking.

→ *The World Bank will support social funds in becoming integral to community-driven development and will* *improve project design and implementation to better address vulnerability.*

Other Support for Informal Risk Management

Family-based risk management is common throughout much of the world, but it has costs. In traditional societies, strong leadership by the head of the household or extended family often characterizes the risk management situation, consequently leaving women and children in a weak position. Thus, some mitigation mechanisms, such as forced marriage, can be detrimental to development. In industrialized societies, household or family members can claim risk sharing and income support through laws enforced by tribunals, which incidentally create incentives and reactions of their own. Given these tensions, what are the possibilities and limits of government action to strengthen informal arrangements while keeping the negative aspects in check? Two areas have been identified as especially important: (a) increasing access to the right to own and build assets, and (b) supporting community-based care for the critically vulnerable (see, for example, "Dynamic Risk Management and the Poor: Developing a Social Protection Strategy for Africa," World Bank 2000).

Extending the Right to Own Assets. In the area of informal risk mitigation, individuals and households need to build up their assets in order to optimize their portfolio. However, there are often serious social and legal restrictions on the rights to build up assets, especially for women. In many parts of the world, women cannot inherit assets from their deceased husbands (in some countries, they do not even inherit their own children). In others, women are barred from owning land or having their own savings accounts, forcing them to use more illiquid assets such as jewelry. Important public actions to change this could include the following:

■ Legal reform to extend property rights, especially to productive assets such as land and housing, including land titling and revised cadastres—this may also require specific measures to ensure that banks and other financial institutions will accept women's property title as collateral.[5]
■ Legal assistance and legal literacy programs, especially for women and marginalized groups (such as indigenous peoples or minorities), both to educate them on their rights and to help them to obtain access.
■ Assistance to organizations of women and marginalized groups in demanding better services.

COMMUNITY-BASED INSURANCE

Social funds can be designed to combine state interventions with informal insurance mechanisms. In Zimbabwe, for example, the recently operational Community Action Project will provide funding for communal grain storage facilities if required. Under these arrangements, the village chief sets aside a plot of land and the community provides labor for agricultural production. The produce generated is then earmarked for particularly vulnerable households or to meet seasonal or sudden shocks.

Supporting Community-Based Services for the Critically Vulnerable. The AIDS pandemic in Africa (and also threatening South Asia) has created extremely high numbers of orphans, straining the capacities of traditional informal support mechanisms. Compounding this situation is the simultaneous need to care for the dying. Social funds are exploring ways to support these informal mechanisms and build community alliances for AIDS work (in collaboration with UNAIDS). Various programs (for example, giving regular transfers to care-giving grandparents) need to be piloted and modified on the basis of lessons learned. Another major challenge is the institutionalization of the disabled and incapacitated elderly in the Europe/Central Asia region, which has become unsustainable. Lithuania is piloting interesting projects involving community-based approaches, and other countries are considering them. The World Bank can support community services for the critically vulnerable by:

- Expanding the menu of community-based projects to include explicit support for care of the critically vulnerable;
- Quickly applying lessons from the de-institutionalization of pilot projects to other countries; and,

- Piloting and increasing direct support for community-based services, like the Zunde Ramambo scheme in Zimbabwe (Box 5.4).

→ *The World Bank, with its partners, will promote the extension of ownership rights to assets and support community-based services for the critically vulnerable.*

Increasing Poor People's Access to Market-Based Interventions

The difficulties with microcredit in traditional social protection programs have led the World Bank to reduce support for this kind of intervention. Similarly, with regard to microfinance, the World Bank now downplays its social role and emphasizes instead the need to build sustainable financial institutions. Given that financial markets have a role to play in risk management for poor people, the World Bank has an opportunity to start supporting microfinance interventions again, this time on a much more sustainable basis. Promising avenues include building knowledge and support through the following:

- Promoting microsavings within social funds, other community-based mechanisms, nongovernmental organizations' projects, and other social protection programs. This could prepare the way for a gradual move toward microcredit.
- Piloting microinsurance in the form of microsavings and credit institutions, also informally (for example, as is occurring with coconut workers in Sri Lanka).
- Creating links between safety nets and microfinance, for example, linking food rations for poor people with savings (as in Bangladesh).
- Experimenting with microfinance during conflict, natural disasters, and financial crises.

→ *The World Bank will support pilot programs that better integrate social protection interventions with microfinance products, especially microsavings and microinsurance.*

37

NOTES FROM CHAPTER FIVE

[1] Labor market policies obviously have many other objectives beyond social risk management, including the creation of opportunity and empowerment (World Bank 1995). However, what unites labor, old-age income support, and safety nets is that they all contribute to social risk management (as one of their objectives).

[2] The World Bank's recent support to parents in Indonesia to keep their children in school despite the economic crisis is a good example of how a coping intervention can support long-term risk reduction and mitigation (through investment in children's education).

[3] The International Labor Organization has highlighted possibilities for collaboration with the World Bank on these important issues (ILO 1999).

[4] The Pension Reform Primer series summarizes existing knowledge and country experiences, and a research conference in September 1999 highlighted areas of new and innovative thinking (Holzmann and Stiglitz 2001).

[5] For example, Tanzania has taken a number of measures to guarantee that the gender equity clauses in the 1999 Land Law become effective. These measures include legal literacy training and issuance of special certificates to women landowners to ensure that financial institutions will accept their titles.

MOVING FORWARD:

STRATEGIC DIRECTIONS

Based on the social risk management framework, the World Bank proposes to work with external partners to convince policymakers of the importance of risk management to poverty reduction. It will also offer support to governments in implementing specific social protection instruments, or to other sectors in improving their programs' effect on risk management. This process will be demand-driven and characterized by joint learning and piloting in many areas where knowledge is still limited. In some areas the social protection sector has well-tested products (for example, in pension reform and support for community-driven development), while in others the World Bank will use its ability to link up with overall macropolicies or finance the scaling-up of other agencies' pilot efforts. The Bank's social protection sector will also continue to follow the lead of partners when they possess the comparative advantage (in issues such as child labor, for example).

This chapter summarizes the implications for the World Bank of the new social protection strategy (both as a theme and a sector) spelled out in the previous chapters. It explains in greater detail the potential impact on regional work-program priorities, countries of emphasis, the World Bank's products (changes, refinements, and new products), partnerships, and resources, both human and financial.

REGIONAL WORK PROGRAM PRIORITIES

Based on the regional sector strategy work summarized in Annex D, Table 6.1 presents shifts in the World Bank's work program priorities. This exercise assumes significant growth in the allocation to the social protection sector within World Bank country budgets to reflect the increased demand for social protection services. Within the overall strategy outlined in Chapters 4 and 5—more thematic cross-sectoral work, more support for informal and market-based risk management, and re-evaluation of interventions for helping people to manage risk—the priorities for the regions reflect their specific risk profiles and corresponding risk management arrangements.

There will be several shifts in the regional sector strategies according to traditional subsectoral distinctions. The first important shift will entail an expansion in the amount and kind of work done by the social protection sector outside its traditional interventions, as discussed in

Chapter 4. This includes work on poverty reduction strategy papers and country strategy development under the Comprehensive Development Framework, both in the creation of sourcebooks and the application of the "security" dimension of the new WDR 2000/1 framework. In addition, the staff of the social protection sector will work with other World Bank staff (in the legal department and financial sector and rural development groups) to develop better approaches to informal and market-based risk management. Within the Human Development Network, examples of the sector's cross-cutting work include health insurance and AIDS management in the health sector, and skills development in education. In its traditional areas, the sector is likely to do more work on labor markets, child labor, and safety nets, to continue its involvement in pensions and social funds, and to focus on mainstreaming disability and youth issues into the regular work program.

COUNTRIES OF EMPHASIS

Two considerations—importance and opportunity—will help determine the actual translation of the strategic directions into country programs. "Importance" refers to the significance of social risk management problems in a country at both global and country-specific levels. From a global perspective, this appears in two ways: (a) problems in one country may affect other countries' ability to

Table 6.1: The World Bank's Social Protection Priorities by Region

Region	Strategic Directions
Sub-Saharan Africa	Work with other human development sectors to mainstream work on orphans and AIDS/HIV management; other sectors to strengthen community-driven development. Integrate pensions and labor work more fully with the rest of social protection.
East Asia and the Pacific	Help clients to establish sustainable public safety nets, improve functioning of and access to market-based arrangements, and review and support informal safety net arrangements.
Europe and Central Asia	Push strongly on second-generation reforms, better integrate social protection subsectors and establish more community-based activities as a complement to public interventions.
Latin America and the Caribbean	Integrate social risk management into country dialogue, with country papers helping to identify gaps and the need for reform of risk management instruments.
Middle East and North Africa	Improve the functioning of public provisions, the quality of services, and the synergy between governments and civil society in providing social risk management instruments.
South Asia	Establish social risk management as an important element of poverty reduction; focus on microfinance, microinsurance, and pension reform in terms of operations.

manage risk, for instance, through migration, financial contagion, or other spillover effects; and, (b) one country may be exploring innovative solutions that could prove valuable for other countries. The type and scope of the World Bank's involvement will also depend on the degree of interest each country has in addressing social protection issues—in other words, the "opportunity" for World Bank participation.[1]

Table 6.2 presents a conceptual framework useful in determining those countries to which the World Bank should direct most of its attention. Each country can identify a set of services in the table that is most appropriate to its specific circumstances and budget capacity. The "countries of emphasis" (where the Bank is highly involved) would be those that meet the criteria in the first row and column of the table, even though the full array of services would only be found in the "high-intensity" countries.

Sub-Saharan Africa presents special challenges. The risks are numerous, severe, and widespread, while the means and instruments for risk management are limited. This would indicate a need for a special emphasis on the region. However, three constraints limit the opportunity for the sector:

- Issues of vulnerability compete with other priorities for the attention of policymakers.
- Where vulnerability and risks are identified priorities, nonsocial protection instruments (especially basic health and education) provide the best means of dealing with problems such as drought, disease, and civil war in many African countries.
- The capacity to implement social protection instruments is so low (except when done in partnership with communities through social funds) that even if a social protection instrument would be the ideal solution, the costs of providing it may be prohibitively high.

The World Bank will work to convince governments in the Sub-Saharan region that risk management matters for poverty reduction, but this may not guarantee that social protection as a sector will become a top priority in Africa. There is an increased interest in social protection interventions as components of other programs, for example, reforming civil service pensions as part of overall civil service reform. Very recently there have also been requests on a subregional level in several social protection areas, and this may be a promising avenue for support during the later years of the strategy implementation.

STRATEGIC DIRECTIONS BY PRODUCT TYPE

The World Bank's services work best on an integrated basis. However, for presentational purposes, this section will categorize the strategic directions required by the new social protection approach in terms of the World Bank's traditional products and services (see Table 6.3).

Country Strategy Work

The successful implementation of the World Bank's social protection sector strategy will depend on the extent to which countries integrate social protection analysis into their own strategy work.[2] The World Bank's social protection sector will continue to help countries with their Poverty Reduction Strategy Papers (PRSPs) at the macro level, to ensure the incorporation of the issue of security (risk management), and at the sectoral level, to make certain that the analysis and proposed interventions (as outlined in Chapter 4) occur within the new strategic framework. In the relatively less poor countries that do not produce PRSPs, the World Bank will adapt its PRSP Sourcebook for application to Country Economic Memoranda, Poverty Assessments, Social and Structural Reviews, and other analytical work. In countries that do not have these reviews (the "engagement" and "pivot"

countries in Table 6.2), the World Bank will support analytical work upstream in the process of preparing a Country Assistance Strategy (CAS) to highlight the importance of social protection.

Analytical and Advisory Activities

The social protection sector's strategic reorientation will create some changes in the World Bank's analytical and advisory products, including the following:

- More comprehensive and action-oriented economic and sector work and more dynamic poverty assessments. This will involve assessing not just numbers of poor people and their distance from the poverty line, but also their vulnerability and income trajectories, and expanding participatory poverty assessments that include poor people's risk management options and techniques.
- More research. Topics that deserve more research attention include reducing child labor, supporting informal safety nets and "simmering" safety nets that are ready when a crisis hits, developing income support systems for the unemployed and the elderly poor, and increasing the coverage of social protection services and legal protections.

Table 6.2: Potential Role of the World Bank in Social Protection: Framework for Selection

Importance of Social Protection / Opportunity Level for Bank	Important from a country perspective and in terms of potential spillover	Important as potential innovator and less important in terms of spillover	Little global importance
Interest in borrowing and dialogue	**High intensity countries:** Full support for lending, knowledge sharing, and analytical work.	**Learning and innovation countries:** Full-scale support by Regions, emphasis on learning and innovation loans and monitoring and evaluation. Support from Sector Board on quality and knowledge services.	**Regional priority countries:** Diverse support by Regions in analytical and lending work, quality assurance services offered by Sector Board on a demand-driven basis.
Interest in dialogue only	**Pivot countries:** Intensive dialogue, analytical work, major emphasis on upstream work in Country Assistance Strategy.	Limited involvement, only to capture learning from country's experience to the benefit of World Bank client countries.	Minimal or no World Bank involvement.
No interest in World Bank involvement in social protection	**Engagement countries:** Mostly Sector Board resources finance upstream work for Country Assistance Strategy. Mainly analytical work and knowledge sharing, often led by other agencies or other sectors (e.g., UNICEF on children).	Limited involvement, only to capture learning from country's experience to the benefit of World Bank client countries.	No World Bank involvement.

Table 6.3: Changes in World Bank Products Based on New Social Protection Approach

Product	Shifts in Strategy Required by Social Risk Management Approach
Country strategy work	■ Promote risk management as a theme in the overall discussion of poverty reduction ■ Use tools such as the social protection PRSP Sourcebook to encourage the incorporation of social protection instruments into country strategies
Analytical and advisory services	■ Move to more comprehensive and action-oriented sector analyses ■ Improve dynamic vulnerability aspects of poverty assessments, especially from a gender perspective
Portfolio management and quality enhancement	■ Maintain the sector's portfolio in a quality leadership position ■ Evaluate the explosive growth in lending, and rework existing operations against the new risk management benchmark
Knowledge management	■ Expand and maintain reform "primers," which compile current analytical thinking, operational lessons, and case studies into an accessible handbook format
Lending	■ Explore new dissemination technologies ■ Undertake more pilot programs ■ Employ adjustment operations in countries still in need of first-generation sector reform and initiate second-generation reforms ■ Scale up community-driven development based on social funds
Information	■ Support dissemination of the new risk management and social protection communicationapproach, including through the World Development Report 2000/1 and the World BankInstitute
Evaluation	■ Refine evaluation criteria and benchmarks ■ Adjust household surveys to better reflect vulnerability indicators including intra-household data ■ Assess the appropriateness of different risk management instruments

42

Portfolio Management and Quality Enhancement

The highest priority for the sector is to ensure that the lending portfolio remains among the best in the World Bank. This will require significant investments, since the portfolio has expanded very rapidly without a corresponding rise in resource allocations. It is unlikely that the nature of portfolio support will need to change, except to ensure that projects reflect the social risk management framework (especially in terms of monitoring and evaluation). The Sector Board's recent implementation of "quality enhancement reviews" (on-demand quality support reviews) has helped it assume a more proactive role in quality assurance. The Social Protection Sector Board is now in a position to judge all projects on how they help poor people manage risk, using this strategy paper as a benchmark. However, many critical questions remain, such as how to measure vulnerability and how to balance coping, reduction, and mitigation strategies. In the area of labor market and training projects, the portfolio may need to be restructured as the World Bank generates new knowledge and begins to learn from pilot experiences.

Knowledge Management

To ensure that the best available knowledge is applied to the World Bank's products to maximize their impacts, the social protection sector has found two approaches especially important.

■ Expanding and maintaining reform primers. The Social Protection Sector Board has pioneered work on reform "primers" in the pension area. Each report in the Pension Reform Primer series brings together current analytical thinking, operational lessons, and case studies into a flexible and accessible handbook format. Over the next three years the World Bank's social protection sector staff hope to maintain and update the Pension Reform Primer series and complete new primers on labor market interventions, safety nets, social funds, and child labor.

- Exploring new technologies for dissemination. The Sector Board, together with the World Bank Institute and the Development Economics research group, will support conferences and knowledge dissemination via the Internet. It will also seek the collaboration and support of regional networks of practitioners, such as the regional social funds networks.

Lending

Overall, successful implementation of this strategy will mean lower annual lending amounts. This is because the social protection sector of the World Bank will generate more but smaller projects from which it can pilot and learn, since the need for large-scale first-generation reforms and crisis lending is subsiding. Other considerations for lending include the following.

- Piloting new approaches in traditional areas. The social protection sector staff will develop and implement a series of pilot learning and innovation loans.[3] Based on the outcome, the use of other lending instruments may be appropriate, including sector investment loans and adaptable program loans.

- Reorienting adjustment lending for first-generation reforms. The sector will continue to use adjustment loans to facilitate the initial "stroke of the pen" reforms (where there is mainly need for legal or regulation changes requiring few or no institutional reforms). Likely options for future adjustment loans include redressing the overloaded formal (mainly public sector) social protection programs in Africa and other low-income countries, establishing appropriate safety nets, moving labor market reforms beyond a simple "markets know best" approach, and initiating legal reforms to strengthen property rights (especially for women). If crises re-emerge, the social protection sector will be ready and able to raise its crisis lending quickly based on its recent experience (see Chapter 2, Guiding Principles).

- Using more flexible investment loans for second-generation reforms and for scaling up social funds. A second generation of pension reforms, especially in Eastern Europe and Latin America, will require even more collaboration and stronger implementation support as the World Bank moves into areas that are politically difficult, require more institutional reform, and in which knowledge is limited. This will likely involve greater use of programmatic lending instruments that allow for an adaptable medium-term approach to policy reforms with step-by-step capacity building, such as programmatic structural adjustment loans and credits, and adaptable program loans and credits. Similarly, many social funds are likely to be scaled up to cover the whole country through the use of Adaptable Program Loans, as part of the overall community-driven development agenda.

Information and Communication

In collaboration with its development partners, the World Bank's social protection sector will continue to focus on the importance of managing risk and insecurity to reduce poverty. Special efforts will be required in presenting this vision of social protection to policymakers and to broaden their view of social protection, especially regarding its links to macroeconomic policy. The World Bank Institute and the World Bank's external affairs department will be critical internal partners in this area. The World Bank Institute has already incorporated elements of the new view of social protection into training courses for African academics and into its core courses in pensions, labor, and safety nets (the last two still under development).

Evaluation

Evaluation has been relatively limited so far. The introduction of social risk management will reshape the way the World Bank thinks about assessments and will require:

- Developing appropriate indicators for risk management and vulnerability at the household and community levels;

- Working across the sector group with units involved in research, such as the Development Economics Vice-Presidency, to adjust the format of the living standard measurement surveys and to support the collection of more household and community-based panel data;[4]

- Encouraging the Operations Evaluation Department to assess the appropriateness of various instruments in preventing, mitigating, and coping with crises (a planned evaluation of social funds would benefit from the incorporation of the risk management framework); and

- Expanding the use of beneficiary assessments.

PARTNERSHIPS

It will become increasingly important for the World Bank to work with partners in the area of social risk management. The Comprehensive Development Framework process will be critical in building partnerships with other development agencies on the World Bank's social protection strategy. On the conceptual front, a consensus is already emerging among several key actors on a framework similar to social risk management (see Box 6.1).

In forming partnerships in the area of social protection, the World Bank's generic principles for partnerships should apply.[5]

■ It is best to set up operational partnerships in a given country setting under an overall agreement to cooperate among the agencies, while it is best to establish knowledge partnerships on a global level.

■ Partnerships should be founded on a division of labor corresponding to the partners' comparative advantages in terms of output.

■ While partnerships are important, they are costly to establish and maintain, so it is necessary to review them periodically to ensure that their positive impact on country programs justifies their costs.

Governments must take the lead in implementing many of the measures outlined in Chapters 4 and 5, but for these measures to be successful, other actors will also have to be involved, including the private sector and civil society. This calls for taking stock of partnerships in light of partners' current and planned activities, and setting priorities. In this process, the social protection sector proposes to consider partnerships according to three dimensions: type of content, type of cooperation, and type of partner, as outlined in Table 6.4.

Partnership by type of content falls into three main categories: knowledge management, which includes the creation, absorption and dissemination of relevant processed information; training and institution building, which involves training in toolkits, regional workshops on pension or labor market issues, and social fund practitioner networks; and operational work, which encompasses all lending and other nonlending services. These three types of partnerships can be thought of in terms of the level of interaction: knowledge management occurs largely at the global level, training and institution building at the regional level, and operational work at the country level.

Partnerships can also be distinguished by the level of cooperation they entail. Table 6.4 specifies three main levels of cooperation: information exchange, coordination

---

BOX 6.1

SIMILARITIES IN PARTNER AND WORLD BANK CONCEPTS

The United Nations Development Program (UNDP) has recently embarked on a Global Program on Sustainable Livelihoods, formulated as a response to the 1995 World Summit for Social Development. The UNDP's approach is, in turn, based on the sustainable livelihood approaches of the Institute for Development Studies, and the International Institute for Sustainable Development, which focused attention on how households use their assets to smooth their income and consumption and reduce vulnerability (Singh and Gilman 1999). The UNDP is already beginning to introduce its sustainable livelihood approach in several countries. The United Kingdom's Department for International Development has also embraced the sustainable livelihood approach and has organized a Sustainable Livelihood Resource Group. It recently held a workshop in which emerging approaches across a spectrum of donor agencies (ILO, World Bank, Department for International Development, and Asian Development Bank) showed great similarities, as summarized by de Haan (in Conway and others 2000):

"...various international development agencies have slightly different understandings of what social protection is. But two issues are common. First, it emphasizes risk and vulnerability. This recognizes the dynamic nature of poverty, and—not least as a result of recent crises like in East Asia—focuses our attention on the need to be prepared for crises. This should help us toward a proactive social policy agenda, one that—as put forward in the World Bank framework—emphasizes the need to assist individuals, households, and communities to manage risk and increase security. Second, a social protection framework emphasizes the need to provide support to the poorest."

Source: Conway and others 2000

of activities, and active collaboration. These forms of cooperation are important in terms of budgetary implications. Information exchange often involves low or zero costs, especially with the advent of current technology such as websites and e-mail. Coordination of activities involves low or moderate costs, resulting essentially from prior analysis and transaction costs of communication. Collaboration involves moderate to high costs, since joint secretariats need to be established and resources must be committed to activities.

Finally, Table 6.4 divides the World Bank's potential partners into five main categories: international financial and development institutions; United Nations System organizations (including ILO and UNICEF); multilateral knowledge institutions and sponsors; bilateral donor institutions; and civil society organizations (most importantly trade unions and NGOs).

The preceding analysis of partnerships sets the stage for the decisionmaking process and assists in the identification of strategic implications, as shown in Table 6.4.

Table 6.4: Partnerships and Strategic Directions

Partners	Knowledge Management	Training and Institution Building	Operational Work
International Financial Institutions			
International Monetary Fund	Continued collaboration on Social Protection PRSPs		Selective collaboration on countries' pension reforms
Regional development banks	Enhanced information exchange	Pension reform training with Asian Development Bank Institute	Strengthened coordination on country operations with focus on Africa
United Nations System			
International Labor Organization	Continued information exchange and cooperation in child labor, labor market, and pension areas	Collaboration in social protection training	Collaboration in social expenditure reviews and envisaged collaboration in actuarial services
United Nations Children's Fund (UNICEF)	Cooperation in child labor protection		Cooperation in child labor protection and community-driven development
UNDP, Social Commission, etc.	Enhanced information exchange		Enhanced information exchange
Bilateral Donors			
Various bilateral donors	Enhanced information exchange	Training and capacity building through World Bank Institute and project activities	Selective collaboration at country level on implementing social risk management
Knowledge Partners			
OECD and ISSA	Continued information exchange		Potential cooperation on ICT in social protection with ISSA
European Union Commission	Enhanced information exchange		Strengthened collaboration on EU accession countries
Civil society			
Trade unions and employer's associations	Continued information exchange on core labor standards with global trade union organizations (ICFTU, WCL)	Continued seminars for trade union leaders, and seminars for Bank staff on trade unions	Continued information exchange with trade unions at country level
Nongovernmental Organizations	Enhanced information exchange		Selective cooperation on country basis on CDD and child labor

Notes: This table distinguishes three main types of cooperation: (a) exchange of information in all three content areas—knowledge management, training and institution building, and operations work; (b) coordination of activities (division of labor); and (c) collaboration in activities (joint products).

While the World Bank's social protection sector has significant and improved information exchanges with the International Monetary Fund, the Asian Development Bank, and the International Labor Organization, progress has been slower with other potential partners. In particular, the social protection sector should strengthen information sharing with the other regional development banks, the United Nations organizations (especially the United Nations Development Program and the Commission of Social Development), bilateral donors, and nongovernmental organizations. This is necessary before considering higher levels of cooperation, and it also explains why more expensive collaboration activities are not fully developed. Coordination efforts will be enhanced for operational work, mainly with the regional development banks and bilateral donors. Full collaboration is now concentrated on a few items and often financed through trust funds (for example, work with the ILO/UNICEF on child labor, and with the ILO on labor market issues in East Asia). The envisaged extension of collaboration in training and operational work is selective and in line with restricted budgetary allocations.

RESOURCE IMPLICATIONS

As the loan portfolio of the World Bank's social protection sector ages and grows over the next five to seven years, maintaining the level of quality and addressing the deficiencies in monitoring and evaluation will require rising investments, especially since the value of resources per dollar lent today is around one-third of the value three years ago. In addition, the sector strategy proposed in this paper, if fully implemented, implies the need for additional resources on top of those needed to maintain the quality of the rapidly growing portfolio.

In light of the experience of other World Bank sectors facing resource limitations, if the budget for the social protection sector were to remain flat, the sector would implement a "portfolio first" strategy, concentrating on maintaining the quality of existing projects before generating new ones. Analytical and advisory activities would have to be limited to providing inputs into cross-sectoral work as required by the Comprehensive Development Framework and the overall country dialogue. Geographically, the social protection sector would focus first on the "high-intensity" countries and expand to other "countries of emphasis" only as resources increase. The sector would maintain very limited partnerships and only embark on more expensive partnerships (such as

those with trade unions) as additional resources became available.

With the shift in emphasis toward social risk management, there will be a need to build up the sector's staff skills in broad risk management analysis and action. In other words, the sector will need to acquire or develop social protection specialists.[6] Staff members will increasingly be expected to understand the social risk management framework and to apply it outside their own subsector. In addition, a limited number of specialists in areas such as social protection administration and information technology will be required.

Besides recruitment, the social protection sector staff will need to train other World Bank staff in how to use the social risk management framework for analytical and operational work. The WBI is working on a series of core courses on labor, safety nets, and pensions, each of which will have an overarching social risk management session showing the framework's links with the agenda beyond the traditional definition of social protection. In addition, the sector's current practice of sponsoring seminars on conceptual issues and evolving operational practice will continue. The Sector Board is expected to expand its nontraditional forms of training, including mentoring and apprenticeships.

LOOKING FORWARD

Social policy issues became increasingly important throughout the 1990s. As the development community recognized that economic growth alone was not enough to guarantee lasting poverty reduction, it increasingly emphasized social policies and appropriate social protection instruments, given their role in achieving inclusive growth. Similar changes in focus within the World Bank have led to a sharp rise in both the lending and nonlending services in the area of social protection.

At the beginning of this new century, development practitioners are realizing that, while individual programs can improve people's welfare and reduce poverty, a more holistic approach is needed to make the quantum leaps necessary to lift most poor people in the developing world out of poverty. Many agencies are rethinking or developing their strategies for social protection using comprehensive frameworks that emphasize both risk and redistribution, such as the social risk management strategy presented in this paper. The approaches are sufficiently similar to allow for good collaboration, while sufficiently different to accommodate the varying objectives of the agencies, thereby creating a particularly appropriate environment for the creation of partnerships.

The World Bank's Comprehensive Development Framework reflects this more holistic understanding. This Social Protection Sector Strategy Paper follows this lead by broadening the definition of social protection to encompass any public intervention that helps individuals, households, and communities manage risk and that provides support to the critically poor.

The strategy outlined in this paper will help the World Bank to be a credible partner in worldwide social policy development in the following ways:

- Participating actively in the followup to June 2000 Global Social Summit in Geneva, and in any events related to it, under the leadership of the social development group of the World Bank.
- Supporting the United Nations Commission of Social Development as it prepares to make social protection the central theme of its 2001 session.

- Applying the work done under the Poverty Reduction Strategy Paper Sourcebooks to the continued development of good practice on social policy (the "social principles") under the leadership of the United Nations.
- Assisting in the dissemination of the "security" aspects of the World Development Report 2000/1 as consistent with this strategy paper.

The next stage of this strategy, developing partnerships and a common approach to social policy within a global vision of poverty reduction, will be the true test of whether the World Bank's mission statement is to become a reality.

Our dream is a world free of poverty.

NOTES FROM CHAPTER SIX

[1] More specifically, this refers to the interest the country has in social protection as compared to other sectors.

[2] Pilots of a three-stage application of the social risk management framework are proving very promising in helping various Latin American countries—including Argentina, Jamaica, Dominican Republic and Uruguay—to include social protection in the CAS process. Stage one identifies the main risks in the country, particularly those to which poor people are exposed. Stage two reviews the available risk management arrangements—informal, market-based, and public—and their role and effectiveness for risk prevention, mitigation, and coping. Finally, stage three develops with the country the priority and sequence of actions necessary to close the gap between risk-determined need and social protection instruments. It also determines the urgency and timing for the reform and introduction or expansion of social protection interventions.

[3] Areas identified in the regional strategy papers include: support for coping with the AIDS pandemic, new approaches to caring for orphans, and the integration of microfinance (especially savings) into social protection programs.

[4] The regions and Sector Board would provide resources to support these activities.

[5] This section uses as an important reference the new approach to partnership oversight and selectivity recently outlined by the World Bank (2000d).

[6] The social protection sector will work with the overall Human Development Network in its efforts to strengthen the base of economists and other social scientists among network staff.

(Note: The word "processed" at the end of certain entries describes informally reproduced works that may not be commonly available through libraries.)

Alwang, J., and P.B. Siegel. 2000. "Towards Operational Definitions and Measures of Vulnerability: A Review of the Literature from Different Disciplines." Social Protection Unit. World Bank, Washington, D.C. September. Processed.

Anker, R. 1998. *Gender and Jobs: Sex Segregation of Occupations in the World.* International Labour Office, Geneva.

Badelt, C. 1999. *Social Risk Management and Social Inclusion.* World Bank, Washington, D.C. Processed.

Bernstein, P. 1996. *Against the Gods—The Remarkable Story of Risk.* New York: John Wiley and Sons.

Bigio, A., ed. 1998. "Social Funds and Reaching the Poor: Experiences and Future Directions." Proceedings prepared for an International Workshop on Social Funds, May 21-24, World Bank, Washington, D.C.

Case, A., and A. Deaton. 1996. "Large Cash Transfers to the Elderly in South Africa." Working Paper 5572. National Bureau of Economic Research, Cambridge, MA.

Castel, P., and L. Fox. 2001. "Gender Dimensions of Pension Reform in the Former Soviet Union." In R. Holzmann and J. Stiglitz, eds., *New Ideas About Old Age Security.* Proceedings of the World Bank's Pension Reform Research Conference, September 1999 (in preparation).

Conway, T., A. de Haan, R. Holzmann, S. Jorgensen, A. Norton, I. Ortiz, and W. van Ginneken. 2000. "Social Protection: New Directions of Donor Agencies." Papers arising from an Inter-Agency Workshop, Easthampstead Park, United Kingdom, 22nd-23rd March 2000.
Dar, A., and Z. Tzannatos. 1999a. "Active Labor Market Programs: A Review of the Evidence from Evaluations." Social Protection Discussion Paper No. 9901. World Bank, Washington, D.C.

———. 1999b. "World Bank Lending for Labor Markets: 1991-1998." Social Protection Discussion Paper No. 9902. World Bank, Washington, D.C.

de Ferranti, D., G. E. Perry, I. S. Gill, and L. Servén. 2000. *Securing Our Future in a Global Economy.* World Bank, Washington, D.C.

Dollar, D. and R. Gatti. 1999. "Gender Inequality, Income, and Growth: Are Good Times Good for Women?" Working Paper Series 1, Policy Research Report on Gender and Development. World Bank, Development Research Group/Poverty Reduction and Economic Management Network, Washington, D.C.

Elson, D. 1991. "Gender Analysis and Economics in the Context of Africa." Manchester Discussion Papers in Development Studies, 9103. University of Manchester, United Kingdom.

Fallon, P., and Z. Tzannatos. 1998. "Child Labor: Issues and Directions for the World Bank." World Bank, Washington, D.C.

Fretwell, D.H., J. Benus, and C.J. O'Leary. 1999. "Evaluating the Impact of Active Labor Programs: Results of Cross-Country Studies in Europe and Central Asia." Social Protection Discussion Paper No. 9915. World Bank, Washington, D.C.

49

Gill, I., F. Fluitman, and A. Dar., eds. 2000. *Vocational Education and Training Reform: Matching Skills to Markets and Budgets.* A Joint Study of the World Bank and International Labour Office. New York: Oxford University Press.

Goodman, M., S. Morley, G. Siri, and E. Zuckerman. 1997. "Social Investment Funds in Latin America: Past Performance and Future Role." Inter-American Development Bank, Evaluation Office, Social Programs and Sustainable Development Department, Washington, D.C.

Grosh, M. 1994. *Administering Targeted Social Programs in Latin America: From Platitudes to Practice.* World Bank, Washington, D.C.

Hill, A. and E. King. 1995. "Women's Education and Economic Well-Being." *Feminist Economics* 1(2): 1-26.

Holzmann, R. 2000. "The World Bank Approach to Pension Reform." *International Social Security Review* 53(1): 11-34.

Holzmann, R., and S. Jorgensen. 1999. "Social Protection as Social Risk Management: Conceptual Underpinnings for the Social Protection Sector Strategy Paper." Journal of International Development 11: 1005-1027.

———. 2000. "Social Risk Management: A New Conceptual Framework for Social Protection and Beyond." Social Protection Discussion Paper No. 0006. World Bank, Washington, D.C.

Holzmann R., and J. Stiglitz, eds. 2001. *New Ideas About Old-Age Security,* Proceedings of the World Bank's Pension Reform Research Conference, September 1999.

Holzmann, R., I. W. Mac Arthur, and Y. Sin. 2000. "Pension Systems in East Asia and the Pacific: Challenges and Opportunities." Social Protection Discussion Paper No. 0014. World Bank, Washington, D.C.

Horton, S., R. Kanbur, and D. Mazumdar. 1994. *Labor Markets in an Era of Adjustment.* World Bank, Economic Development Institute, Washington, D.C.

International Labor Organization (ILO). 1999. *Report of the Director General: Decent Work.* Geneva.

International Monetary Fund (IMF)/International Development Association (IDA). 1999. "HIPC Initiative—Strengthening the Link between Debt Relief and Poverty Reduction." Washington, D.C. Processed.

James, E. 1998. "New Models for Old-Age Security: Experiments, Evidence, and Unanswered Questions." *The World Bank Research Observer* 13(2), August. Washington, D.C.

Jorgensen, S., and J. Van Domelen. 2000. "Helping the Poor Manage Risk Better: The Role of Social Funds." In N. Lustig, ed. *Shielding the Poor: Social Protection in the Developing World.* The Brookings Institution and the Inter-American Development Bank, Washington, D.C.

Klasen, S. 1999. "Does Gender Inequality Reduce Growth and Development? Evidence from Cross-Country Regressions." Working Paper Series 7, Policy Research Report on Gender and Development. World Bank, Development Research Group/Poverty Reduction and Economic Management Network, Washington, D.C.

Owen, D., and J. Van Domelen. 1998. "Getting an Earful: A Review of Beneficiary Assessments of Social Funds." Social Protection Discussion Paper No. 9816. World Bank, Washington, D.C.

Prescott, N. 1999. "Korea Crisis Response." World Bank, Washington, D.C. Processed.

Ravallion, M. 1999. "Protecting the Poor in a Crisis— and Beyond." PREM Notes #12, January. World Bank, Washington, D.C.

Rawlings, L., L. Sherburne-Benz, and J. Van Domelen. 2000. "Evaluating Social Fund Performance Across Countries: Recent Findings and Impact Evaluation Results." World Bank, Washington, D.C. Draft report. Processed.

Sabel, C., D. O'Rourke, and A. Fung. 2000. "Ratcheting Labor Standards: Regulation for Continuous Improvement in the Global Workplace." Social Protection Discussion Paper No. 0011. World Bank, Washington, D.C.

Sayed, H., and D. Filmer. 1998. "The Impact of Indonesia's Economic Crisis on Basic Education: Findings from a Survey of Schools." World Bank, Washington, D.C. Processed.

Siegel, P.B., and Alwang, J. 1999. "An Asset Based Approach to Social Risk Management—A Conceptual Framework." Social Protection Discussion Paper 9926. World Bank, Washington, D.C.

Singh, N., and J. Gilman. 1999. "Making Livelihoods More Sustainable." United Nations Development Program. New York, November. Processed.

Sinha, S., and M. Lipton. 1999. "Undesirable Fluctuations, Risk and Poverty: A Review." World Bank, Washington, D.C., October. Processed.

Smith, L., and L. Haddad. 2000. "Explaining Child Malnutrition in Developing Countries: a Cross-Country Analysis." Discussion Paper No. 60. Food Consumption and Nutrition Division, International Food Policy Research Institute, Washington, D.C.

Subbarao, K., and others. 1997. *Safety Net Programs and Poverty Reduction: Lessons from Cross-Country Experience.* World Bank, Washington, D.C.

United Nations International Children's Education Fund (UNICEF). 1987. *Adjustment with a Human Face: Protecting the Vulnerable and Promoting Growth.* New York: Oxford University Press.

Vodopivec, M. 2000. "Income Support Systems for Unemployed Workers: Issues and Options." World Bank, Social Protection Team, Washington, D.C. Processed.

Wolfensohn, J. D. 1997. "The Challenge of Inclusion." The World Bank Annual Meetings Address. Hong Kong, South Asia Region, China, September 23.

World Bank. 1990. *World Development Report 1990: Poverty.* New York: Oxford University Press.

———. 1999. "A Proposal for a Comprehensive Development Framework (Discussion Draft)." Memorandum from the President, January 21. World Bank, Washington, D.C.

———. 1992. Poverty Reduction Handbook. Washington, D.C.

———. 1994. *Averting the Old-Age Crisis: Policies to Protect the Old and Promote Growth.* New York: Oxford University Press.

———. 1995. *World Bank Development Report 1995: Workers in an Integrating World.* New York: Oxford University Press.

———. 1996. *World Development Report 1996: From Plan to Market.* New York: Oxford University Press.

———. 1998. *East Asia: The Road to Recovery.* Washington, D.C.

———. 1999a. "Building Poverty Reduction Strategies in Developing Countries." Development Committee. Washington, D.C. Processed.

———. 1999b. "Principles and Good Practice of Social Policy: Issues and Areas for Public Actions." World Bank for the World Bank/IMF Development Committee, April, Washington, D.C. Processed.

———. 1999c. "Vietnam Draft Poverty Report." Hanoi. Processed.

———. 2000a. "Community-Driven Development Draft Principles." Washington, D.C. Processed.

———. 2000b. "Engendering Development." Policy Research Report (consultation draft). Washington, D.C.

———. 2000c. *East Asia: Recovery and Beyond.* Washington, D.C.

———. 2000d. "Partnership Oversight and Selectivity and Addressing Global Dimensions in Development (Discussion Notes)." Washington, D.C. Processed.

———. 2000e. "Poverty Reduction Strategy Paper Sourcebook." Washington, D.C. Processed.

———. 2000f. World Development Report 2000/1: Attacking Poverty. New York: Oxford University Press.

Regional Social Protection Sector Strategies

——. 1999. "Managing Social Risk in Latin America and the Caribbean." Presentation by Ana Maria Arriagada, Sector Manager. World Bank, Latin America and Caribbean Region, Washington, D.C.

——. 1999. "Towards an East Asian Social Protection Strategy." (draft) World Bank, East Asia and the Pacific Region, Washington, D.C.

World Bank. 2000. "Dynamic Risk Management and the Poor: Developing a Social Protection Strategy for Africa." (draft) World Bank, Africa Region, Washington, D.C.

——. 2000. *Balancing Protection and Opportunity: A Strategy for Social Protection in Transition Economies.* World Bank, Europe and Central Asia Region, Washington, D.C.

——. 2000. "Risk Management and Poverty: Toward a Social Protection Strategy for South Asia." (draft) World Bank, South Asia Region, Washington, D.C.

——. 2000. "Reducing Vulnerability and Increasing Opportunity: A Strategy for Social Protection in the Middle East and North Africa." World Bank, Middle East and North Africa Region, Washington, D.C.

WORLD BANK INVOLVEMENT

IN PENSION REFORM

The World Bank has played a prominent role in shaping the global debate on pension systems, especially since its publication in October 1994 of *Averting the Old Age Crisis: Policies to Protect the Old and Promote Growth.* This study examined social security provision in terms of its impact on the economy, as well as its role in supporting the elderly. It recommended a "multipillar" system that could confer advantages in efficiency, growth, transparency, and risk diversification. Since this time, the World Bank has actively assisted countries in the design and implementation of such systems. This annex briefly reviews the multipillar pension model, the World Bank approach to pension reform, products it has developed to assist countries, experience in lending for pension reform, and key topics on the agenda in upcoming years.

THE MULTIPILLAR SYSTEM

The multipillar approach consists of three different pension strategies. The foundation pillar, commonly referred to as the second pillar, is a mandatory fully funded, defined contribution system under private and competitive management, but well regulated by public authorities. It involves contributions by individuals, at a legislated rate, that are invested by a fund management authority to earn a high risk-adjusted rate of return. The individual pension comes from the accumulated funds upon retirement. By contrast, traditional pay-as-you-go (PAYG) systems take contributions from workers based on a future promise to pay a fixed percentage of final salary (defined benefit) during retirement. However, they use the revenue right away to pay current pensioners, leaving open the question of whether the promise is sustainable. Thus, funded systems hold some advantages over traditional systems. The second pillar would be able to provide better income replacement for a given contribution rate (particularly given an aging population), help insulate against political risk associated with public pension systems, enhance national savings, promote capital market development, and reduce labor market distortions by linking contributions to benefits.

On the other hand, a defined contribution system cannot protect the poor against poverty in old age since they may be unable to save sufficiently to guarantee a livable pension. For this reason, it is essential to include another pillar, commonly referred to as the first pillar,

which consists of a publicly run system financed on a PAYG basis from payroll taxes or the overall revenue base. It could be part of a more general social assistance strategy, comprise a specific old-age social assistance strategy, target only the poor who were contributors during their working years, or provide flat pensions to all contributors or persons over a given age.

Finally, a third pillar of voluntary savings complements the first two pillars. This system acknowledges that anything mandatory will not be optimal for all people. Some people will prefer to save a lot during their working years and consume more during their retirement years. Others will prefer to consume more during their working years and less during their retirement years. If the two mandatory pillars are kept reasonably small, providing moderate income replacement only, then there will be room for this voluntary pillar, which could enjoy tax advantages but would not necessarily be subject to the same draconian regulation possibly required of the mandatory funded pillar.

THE WORLD BANK APPROACH
TO PENSION REFORM

The environment for pension reform differs dramatically among countries, in terms of both starting conditions (such as the inherited system and the stage of financial market developments) and implementation capacity. This implies that no two reforms will be exactly alike. Furthermore, even the best technically prepared pension reform runs the risk of failure if it does not reflect country preferences or if it lacks credibility among the population. In this sense, the preparation of a pension reform plan has to be done by the politicians and technicians within the country itself. Outsiders, such as World Bank staff, can provide advice based on worldwide experience, but ownership and public support must come from the client country. This requires flexibility and innovation rather than the mere application of blueprints.

As a result, the World Bank reacts flexibly to country preferences and circumstances and has supported different reform approaches in different countries. The Bank does not support all proposed reforms, however. There is too much at stake for current and future retirees, and a country as a whole, to engage in a pension reform that is likely to fail in social and economic terms. The World Bank has four key concerns in working with clients on pension policy: (a) short-term financing and long-term viability; (b) effects on economic growth; (c) adequacy and other distributional issues; and (d) political risk. Moreover, it uses several criteria to judge the soundness of a reform proposal: (a) distributive effects; (b) the nature of the macro and fiscal policy environment; (c) capacity of the administrative structure to operate a multipillar system; and (d) the soundness of regulatory and supervisory arrangements.[1]

WORLD BANK COUNTRY ASSISTANCE

With this approach in mind, the World Bank has been formally involved in some form of pension work in approximately 60 countries over the past 15 years, with a full range of products and services. These include lending, analytical and advisory activities, and generation and dissemination of knowledge (for example, training, conferences, study tours, and application of specialized computer applications). The use of these tools has evolved over time in the different regions of the world, as is especially evident in the lending portfolio.

In addition to its financial products, the World Bank has provided formal nonlending services and outputs. Economic and sector work for 31 countries resulted in 42 reports related to pensions. The World Bank also produced 39 publications and 8 network papers covering pension-related issues in 25 and 7 countries, respectively. There were 53 publications and 13 network papers of a thematic or regional nature. The country-specific World Bank reports evaluating pension strategy range from those strictly addressing pension reform issues, such as for the Philippines and China, to country economic reports and

---

BOX A.1

PROST AND THE PENSION PRIMER

The Pension Reform Options Simulation Toolkit (PROST) is a computer application developed by the World Bank that allows for quantitative analysis and modeling of pension systems useful for decision-making regarding reform strategies. The model can project indicators useful in evaluating pension systems, such as implicit pension debt, current fund balances, and fund reserves. It first became available in July 1997, and has subsequently undergone a series of improvements. PROST is useful to a wide array of actors including government officials, policymakers, and World Bank specialists, and demand for the model has been extremely high.

The World Bank's Pension Reform Primer series, produced by the social protection anchor unit with many contributions from regional staff, amalgamates country experiences and makes them available in a readable format to both World Bank staff and clients. The Primer contains both country case studies and cross-country papers, exploring themes such as tax treatment of funded pensions. Topical papers are also available in short notes that are readily accessible to the non-pension professional. However, there are still many issues for which there is no academic body of wisdom, or for which best practices in terms of implementation have yet to be defined. The anchor unit's work program this year focuses on three of the most critical of these issues: coverage, annuities, and administrative costs.

For more information on both products, see www.worldbank.org/pensions.

---

public expenditure reviews containing chapters analyzing pension systems, such as for Tunisia and Estonia. Policy research working papers and other World Bank papers have examined pension system reform in countries including Argentina, Bolivia, Brazil, China, Colombia, Costa Rica, Namibia, Peru, Ukraine, and Zambia.

However, World Bank involvement in pension reform is not limited to lending or the production of formal reports. The World Bank is also committed to activities in the area of knowledge management. It has held informational seminars in China, for example, organized study tours for Koreans, arranged for technical assistance through consultant trust funds in Latvia,[2] and provided training on the Pension Reform Options Simulation Toolkit (PROST) pension model (Box A1) to participants from Kenya, Tanzania, Zambia, the Philippines, Ecuador, Brazil, Russia, and Thailand, among many other countries. Some countries have asked the World Bank to provide informal assistance or conduct evaluations of their pension systems that resulted only in the production of an *aide mémoire*. Out of headquarters, the World Bank has offered multiple conferences (most recently the conference "New Ideas about Old-Age Security"), a yearly Harvard Institute for International Development/World Bank Institute workshop on pension reform in Cambridge, a core course on pensions, and the pension primer (Box A.1).

LENDING FOR PENSION REFORM

The World Bank has made 70 loans to 36 countries during the past 15 years in which the entire loan, or a component, financed pension reform activities. The total amount of these loans was almost US$7.5 billion, with approximately US$3.4 billion[3] devoted to pension reform. The loans include 38 structural and sectoral adjustment operations (which promote policy reform), 8 investment projects (involving, for example, acquisition of equipment, training, institutional strengthening, contracting of services, etc.), 22 cases of technical assistance (normally in support of adjustment or investment project implementation), and two new "Learning and Innovation Loans" (designed to create greater flexibility in use of resources).

Since pension reform has taken on a different character in the various regions, so has World Bank involvement in support of the reform efforts. The World Bank's first loans with pension components supported four structural adjustment and technical assistance operations in Panama, Costa Rica, and Uruguay in the mid-1980s. Since then, there have been an additional 23 loans in the Latin America and Caribbean region (LAC). The transition from planned to market economies in Eastern Europe and the Former Soviet Union has provided ample opportunities for pension reform, with a total of 35 operations financed by the World Bank since 1990. These started with structural adjustment loans in Poland and Hungary and a labor market adjustment and social protection investment project in the Russian Federation. The other regions have been much less active in pension reform and have requested less World Bank lending assis-

tance, as follows: East Asia and the Pacific (EAP)—three operations; Sub-Saharan Africa (AFR)—three operations; and Middle East and North Africa (MENA)—two operations. With the exception of two fairly "pure" pension reform projects in China, these have generally been financial sector or adjustment operations with pension components.

Although most loans in all regions have been for structural or sectoral adjustment, the World Bank did finance some early technical assistance and investment projects[4], and over time the movement of World Bank clients toward multipillar reforms created chances to focus adjustment loans more directly on pension reform. Multipillar reforms generally involve a full or partial diversion of contribution revenue away from the public pay-as-you-go system toward the funded second pillar. Meanwhile, government must honor commitments to current pensioners and those near retirement. Since pension reform usually takes place when the system is already running deficits, even full contributions are not enough to cover expenditures. In a well-designed reform, once current pensioners (and those soon to retire) have passed out of the system, the system should achieve balance, requiring no further government intervention. Therefore, in this case, pension reform fits the classic investment model, where the country increases current expenditure to gain benefits in the future (a reduction in government costs). At this time, the country can call on World Bank lending to help cover the initial expenditures, with the reduction in future government payments providing the resources to repay the loan.

The first World Bank adjustment loan based purely on pension reform took place in December 1996 to Argentina, quickly followed by operations in Mexico, Peru, Uruguay, and Kazakhstan. The Argentine loan was a follow-up operation to the main pension reform, which involved the cessation of special schemes for civil servants in the provinces and their incorporation into the primary public system. Since the provincial pension funds were mostly in deficit and the civil servants chose to divert some of their contributions to defined-contribution, individual accounts, the government faced a large fiscal burden. The benefit came from the reduction in the provincial deficits and the ability to constrain future liabilities. The Mexican loan helped finance transition costs and improve the regulatory framework for the funded pillar. In Peru, the project loan attempted to improve the efficiency of capital markets and allow for the earmarking of privatization proceeds to cover

57

pension obligations. The project in Uruguay fostered increased efficiency among the second pillar pension fund administrators and promoted the development of the private securities market. Kazakhstan's reform loan follows the classic investment approach described above and will help finance the transition from a PAYG to a fully funded system.

LOOKING FORWARD

The World Bank continually faces new challenges in the implementation of multipillar pension reform because of the relatively recent nature of the concept and the World Bank's position as a leader in the field. In this regard, the World Bank is committed to helping clients and has undertaken an active role in terms of research, production of implementation guidelines, and brokering academic and policy advice for clients[5].

While the shift from PAYG, defined benefit schemes toward fully funded, defined contribution schemes removes labor market distortions, the limited experience to date has shown no substantial movement of labor from the informal to the formal market. Furthermore, in the notional account reforms, which should also improve labor market performance, revenue collection has actually fallen in some cases. From the social risk management point of view, this leaves substantial portions of the population to deal with old age and disability risk through informal mechanisms that may not be uniformly available to all people, such as relying on family. The World Bank is promoting studies to determine who is not covered and why. It can then help design policies to either increase coverage or offer noncontributory schemes to allow better risk management for the uncovered.

Longevity risk, the risk that an individual in retirement will live longer than expected, is fully covered by a PAYG system. However, under a defined contribution system, if the pension is paid in lump sum, the risk is borne by the individual. One means of avoiding the risk is through the purchase of an annuity, in which case the provider of the annuity, an insurance company or a public pension fund, bears the risk, converting the defined contribution

pension to a defined benefit. But, in many of the World Bank's client countries, annuities are available only at extremely high prices or not at all. Some of this may be due to adverse selection, where only the individuals expecting to live long lives choose to purchase annuities, which raises their price, or due to other factors, such as tax treatment of annuity income. The World Bank's studies related to this topic attempt to determine why annuities are not being provided and look for optimal ways of organizing annuities markets.

Another key topic of investigation is that of administrative costs. In the limited sample of countries in which defined contribution systems have been implemented, administrative costs in the new systems have been high and have severely limited net rates of return. The studies thus attempt to determine the reasons for this situation and propose a way to improve it. In this way, the World Bank's clients will get access to the best risk management at lowest cost.

There is also increasing interest in the political economy of reform, for which the evidence and analysis are still in their infancy. The available results provide some guidance for policymakers and the World Bank, but they cannot really answer the two main questions: what starts a pension reform, and what makes it successful? While the rising number of pension reforms undertaken worldwide enhances the information pool and the possibility to discriminate better among competing hypotheses, more data and more research are clearly required.

Finally, as client countries face challenges in the field of pension reform, they generate a series of other topics for continued investigation. These include civil servant pension reform, gender and distributional impact, public pension fund governance, and fiscal sustainability issues with notional accounts. Civil servant pension reform deals not only with old age and disability risk management for civil servants, but also with evaluating whether the design of the civil service pension system involves such heavy subsidies from the government that it precludes other government assistance in social risk management.

NOTES FROM ANNEX ONE

1 See Holzmann, R. (2000): "The World Bank Approach to Pension Reform," *International Social Security Review* 53(1): 11-34.

2 This type of activity often does not lead to lending or the production of a report.

[3] Since most adjustment loans and even some investment loans do not specify the values associated with the different components or policy reform measures, this figure represents a rough estimate. It generally assumes that the typical adjustment loan involving pensions dedicated around 10% to pension reform. When the number of policy reform areas was specified, the estimate for any single component simply resulted from the total loan value divided by the number of components.

[4] In the mid-1990s there were three technical assistance loans to LAC countries and four investment loans to ECA countries concentrating mainly on infrastructural inputs required to accomplish administrative improvements.

[5] For the results of a research conference on "New Ideas About Old-Age Security" in September 1999, jointly sponsored by the Social Protection Unit and the Development Economics Vice-Presidency, see Holzmann and Stiglitz, eds. (2001): *New Ideas About Old-Age Security*, World Bank, Washington, D.C. (forthcoming).

REGIONAL RESEARCH, ANALYTICAL AND ADVISORY ACTIVITIES, AND KNOWLEDGE MANAGEMENT

World Bank staff have carried out research and analytical work over the years to provide the underpinning for World Bank-financed projects as well as knowledge to client countries and the global development community. The Development Economics Vice Presidency has undertaken research on labor markets, pensions, and social assistance for more than two decades. The network anchors (especially for social protection and poverty) generate and disseminate other knowledge products (often thematic or regional in nature) and offer additional services to clients. The World Bank Institute promotes skills and technical capacity building among World Bank staff and clients in areas of social protection. Finally, the World Bank regional units produce the work that is perhaps most directly applicable to operations. This Annex focuses on the main nonlending products and activities of the regions and the linkages between these and the lending portfolio.

EAST ASIA AND THE PACIFIC

Rapid economic growth in many countries in the East Asia and Pacific region (EAP) and a tradition of strong informal (family- and community-based) safety nets gave governments little incentive to plan for downside risks. As a result, formal provision of social protection remained much less common in EAP countries than in those with similar income levels in other regions. Part of the governments' reluctance to establish extensive public social protection interventions resulted from the perception that they would replace informal mechanisms, create dependency, and produce a drag on economic growth. Much of the World Bank's work on social protection in the EAP region has emerged since the region's financial crisis in 1997 and has concentrated on the area of social safety nets. Several countries sought urgent assistance, including both Korea and Malaysia, which had previously graduated from World Bank borrowing. The World Bank put together "emergency" adjustment packages for Indonesia, Korea, Malaysia, the Philippines, and Thailand. Although a large basis of analytical work did not exist before the crisis, the World Bank helped fill the gap while planning responsive measures (See Box B.1 on Korea, which offers an example of close alignment between lending and

nonlending services). The World Bank's *East Asia: The Road to Recovery* report and sequel[1] undertook a comprehensive assessment of the crisis, and the Asia-Europe Meeting (ASEM)-European Union (EU) Financial Crisis Response Fund (ASEM Trust Fund) and Policy and Human Resources Development Grants allowed for the development of 19 more specific inputs. These included seven country and thematic studies on labor markets, five on safety nets, three on pensions, and four on cross-cutting issues. The recent conference, "Labor Markets in the East Asia Crisis: Applied Analysis and Policy Workshop," examined the effects of the crisis on labor markets and policies used to address it.

Before the crisis, the World Bank's social protection portfolio in the region emphasized labor markets above other areas, mainly as a function of country preferences. Support for pension reform has been limited, although economic and sector work has taken on the issue in China, Mongolia, and the Philippines. Interest in social investment funds is increasing, with projects in Cambodia, Indonesia, Lao People's Democratic Republic (PDR), the Philippines, and Thailand. Despite this trend, poverty assessments for the EAP countries are generally outdated. An exception is Thailand, where the 1996

BOX B.1

KOREA—KNOWLEDGE INFORMING ACTION FOR INTEGRATED SOCIAL PROTECTION

The Bank approved an emergency adjustment loan in 1997 and two structural adjustment loans in 1998 for Korea. The loans depended in part on introduction of an integrated social policy agenda. In addition to financing measures to protect pro-poor social expenditures and the unemployed, the lending program included the following actions to upgrade the country's social protection system over the long term:

- **Strengthening the information base for poverty monitoring and targeting;**
- **Improving the unemployment insurance system and related labor market monitoring mechanisms; and**
- **Reforming the pension and health insurance systems.**

The social policy agenda has received support both within the framework of the Structural Adjustment Lending and through technical assistance and other non-lending services. The ASEM program has funded a range of proposals for analytical work on the Korean situation. Finally, a Country Assistance Strategy (CAS) under preparation sets out the planned lending and non-lending activities and their sequencing within a strategic framework.

62

poverty assessment used empirical data to evaluate antipoverty programs and suggested their reorientation to achieve better results. Currently, World Bank staff are preparing poverty updates for Cambodia, Indonesia, Lao PDR, and Papua New Guinea.

To a certain extent, the approach toward social protection among World Bank client countries in the region has differed at a general level according to the following groups: emerging market economies (Indonesia, Korea, Malaysia, the Philippines, and Thailand); transition economies (Cambodia, China, Lao PDR, Mongolia, and Vietnam); and small market economies (Papua New Guinea and the Pacific Islands). Labor market issues have been of special interest to both the emerging market and transition economies because of the continuous need to protect the vulnerable, which the crisis intensified, and the problems posed by redundant labor in the transition. Some of the emerging market economies—Korea, the

Philippines and Thailand—are becoming more concerned with the financial sustainability of their PAYG social security systems, and the same holds true for the transition economies of China, Mongolia, and Vietnam, in which state-owned enterprises have encountered difficulties meeting their obligations. Social safety nets have assumed greater significance after the crisis in the emerging market economies, and social funds are catching on in both emerging market and transition countries. So far, the small market economies have done very little to develop formal social protection interventions, but they face a growing challenge in terms of youth unemployment. In sum, the region bears a large agenda for social protection work, and future advisory and analytical work will likely reflect these subregional priorities.

EUROPE AND CENTRAL ASIA

Prior to the 1990s, most of the current countries in Central and Eastern Europe and Central Asia were not members of the World Bank (except for Yugoslavia, Romania, Hungary after 1982, and Poland after 1986). The World Bank's work on social protection issues in the region was sporadic and related mainly to labor markets and social expenditures, normally in the context of macroeconomic analysis (that is, Country Economic Memoranda). This situation changed dramatically in the early 1990s with the dissolution of the Soviet Union, the entrance of new client countries into the World Bank, and the gradual transition of their economies from central planning to market orientations. The transition spurred the adoption of a new approach toward social protection, which in turn necessitated the restructuring of arrangements and institutions.[2]

Given that the cornerstone of social protection strategy under the socialist system was full employment, the market-oriented transition had rapid and dramatic effects on labor markets, and much of the World Bank's analytical work in the region has focused on this area. Several types of country-specific reports have addressed labor market issues: early Social Sector Reports (for example, Hungary and Romania), Country Economic Memoranda (for example, Slovak Republic), and stand-alone labor market studies (for example, Belarus, Estonia, Kazakhstan, Russian Federation, Slovenia, and Yugoslavia). Complementary regional studies—the most important of which was perhaps *Labor Markets and Social Policy in Central and Eastern Europe*[3]—allowed for a comparative perspective. Papers in the *Social Challenges of Transition* series[4] quantitatively evaluated early transition developments relating to labor market efficiency (such as wage flexibility, hiring and firing restrictions, and collective bargaining) and social protection measures for the unemployed. Many of these sector work pieces used World Bank-sponsored household surveys (for example, the Former Yugoslav Republic (FYR) of Macedonia, Romania, and Russia), in which case the local institutions often benefited from capacity building in this activity.

In some cases there has been close alignment of sector work, a consistent policy dialogue, and subsequent lending. Adjustment operations in Bulgaria, FYR Macedonia, and the Russian Federation gained support from previous or simultaneous investment loans. The coordination between a technical assistance project and a poverty study in FYR Macedonia provides an example of how solid analytical work informed the adjustment lending that followed.

In addition to guaranteed employment, under the socialist system the transition countries provided generous retirement security to workers through fiscally unsustainable PAYG systems. The deterioration of these arrangements under the transition (reflected in a rising system dependency ratio resulting from early retirement, evasion, out migration of labor, greater unemployment and continued population aging) brought urgency to the need for reform. As a result, the World Bank has assisted with the evaluation of problems and reform options. There have been at least 17 official economic and sector work reports addressing pension issues in the region, as well as many other World Bank publications, demonstrating a level of activity comparable to that in the Latin America and Caribbean region. Pension issues often surfaced initially in public expenditure review documents and made up part of adjustment lending packages, to which specific pension reform investment operations provided quick followup. Only four Europe and Central Asia countries have marginal or no relations at all with the World Bank regarding pension reform: Belarus, Tajikistan, Turkmenistan, and Yugoslavia. The ECA region organized several seminars and conferences, including an innovative conference in Vienna in 1998 in which Central and Eastern European reformers facilitated knowledge transfer to policymakers from the Commonwealth of Independent States. In the ECA region, the World Bank also agreed in some cases to temporarily assign its staff to the governments, if requested, to accelerate the transfer of knowledge.

Until now ECA countries have done relatively less with regard to the redesign (or creation) of social safety

nets compared to their reform of labor markets and social insurance. This is largely a consequence of the fact that the socialist system largely precluded development of the full array of market-style safety net structures. The government used extensive subsidies on goods and services to ensure the maintenance of basic needs, provided cash and in-kind benefits for certain vulnerable groups, and emphasized residential care for groups outside the rubric of normal life. The dismantling of the subsidy system, especially in the Eastern European countries, combined with increased unemployment and poverty, neglect of residential institutions, or the significant arrears in cash and in-kind benefits in the Eurasian countries, has meant that social safety nets deserve increasing attention.

The emergency character of protecting the poor during transition has frequently determined the nature of World Bank action in terms of safety nets. This has produced some situations involving a lack of coordination and optimal sequencing among research and lending activities. For example, adjustment interventions have preceded the preparation of poverty assessments, which would have provided an important empirical underpinning for policy planning. Still, in some cases, the country and World Bank have made the best of the circumstances. For example, in 1998 the World Bank funded a sector investment loan in Latvia with the objective of improving the social security delivery system, especially in terms of creating alternatives to institutionalization. Several analytical inputs of interest to program design, including an assessment of the Latvian social assistance system and reform, became available only after project implementation had begun. However, even though the operational activities did not follow an initial poverty assessment and sector work, the World Bank used ongoing analytical work to improve the project under execution.

The most frequent World Bank reports useful to the social safety net area are poverty assessments, which can feed into both policy oriented (adjustment) operations and specific investment projects: for example, social investment funds, which countries of the region are rapidly adopting (such as Albania, Armenia, Bulgaria, Georgia, Moldova, Romania, and Tajikistan). Based on successful projects, the region established the ECA network of social funds, which helps countries exchange information, especially regarding best practices.

Romania provides an especially positive example of comprehensive social protection and safety net programming based on previous analysis. The 1996-97 poverty assessment contributed to the preparation of the following projects: a quick-disbursing Social Protection Adjustment Loan (US$50 million) intended to improve the social safety net, including cash and in-kind benefit programs (June 1997); an investment loan focusing on social services for children, including innovative initiatives to help street children and reduce institutionalization through creation of incentives for home and foster care; and a Social Investment Fund Loan (January 1999). This follows other safety net work, including the World Bank's technical assistance to the Ministry of Labor and Social Protection in the Technical Assistance and Critical Imports Loan (1991) and sector work (1992) that fed into the Employment and Social Protection Project (1995).

In Bulgaria, a Poverty Assessment undertaken in June 1999 found incredibly high rates of poverty among certain disadvantaged ethnic groups such as the Roma. Initially, the government was defensive on this issue, but the dialogue has subsequently led to the development of an Institutional Development Fund Grant on Ethnic Integration (2000), spurred regional analysis on Roma issues (which in turn resulted in a seminal report on the issue for the Prague 2000 meetings), and has contributed to World Bank work on child welfare and the reform of the social assistance system. Sometimes, the linkage has been reversed, and good operations have given rise to sound analytical work and policy advice. A case in point is Bulgaria, where the Social Insurance Administration Project (1995) not only prepared the foundations to implement a multipillar pension reform, but supported the development of the government's analytical capacity to design it, leading to the development of the Social Protection Adjustment Loan in 1998.

Good data are always highly sought after, particularly when they enable cross-country analysis. A major effort has been made through the Social Challenges of Transition (SCT) to compile comparable data on the social sectors throughout all ECA countries. This database has also been linked to the UNICEF Transmonee database, thereby facilitating comparative analysis within the international donor community, amongst academics and within the client country governments.

Child welfare has recently become a major new area in which analytical work is bolstering innovative operations in tackling complex social and developmental problems. Following the 1999 study "Moving from Residential Institutions to Community-Based Services in Eastern Europe and the Former Soviet Union," the World Bank

has become increasingly involved in de-institutionalization, welfare, and human rights issues, particularly among children. Initial efforts in Romania are now being expanded into countries such as Bulgaria, Lithuania, and even Russia.

LATIN AMERICA AND THE CARIBBEAN

Despite differences in socioeconomic development, countries of the Latin America and Caribbean region face a number of common general challenges in social protection and have sought some similar solutions. The countries have sizeable (and growing) informal labor markets (57 percent of workers in 1995 on average, up from 52 percent in 1990), increasing poverty (34-37 percent of the population of the region in the period 1986-96), and very unequal income and asset distributions (Gini in the range of 0.4 to 0.6; on average the highest for any region). Also, some countries have felt the shocks of recent financial and monetary crises (for example, balance of payments and exchange rate) and volatility in foreign investment and private capital flows. Governments have normally established a full range of social protection programs, which have experienced similar difficulties that led to reform. Some countries have been attempting to ease regulation in the formal sector labor market, which has historically driven growth in the informal sector. Fiscal unsustainability of public pension schemes has contributed to widespread experimentation with reform, much of which has followed the multipillar model. Low coverage and inequity from the continued existence of special arrangements for public sector workers in many countries represent some of the unresolved issues in this sector. The region was the first to implement the social investment fund model both as a response to the period of structural adjustment and then as an efficient means to finance and deliver social infrastructure investments. The social investment funds built upon or complemented previously existing safety net programs (mainly in-kind transfer and public employment schemes).

Economic and sector work in the region related to the labor market includes structural reform, unemployment, downsizing and public sector reform, gender, wages and poverty, and training. The performance of labor markets, effects of reform, and prospects for improvements are fundamental areas of investigation.[5] Given the persistent problem of unemployment in some economies, especially in the Caribbean, early country economic memoranda and economic reports often addressed this issue (for example, "Trinidad and Tobago–Report on Employment," 1973; "Barbados–Economic Memorandum," 1986; "Panama–Special Economic Report: Metropolitan Unemployment," 1982). The quality of public administration and governance, which relates to public sector reform, downsizing, and rationalization, has been a prominent concern in the region, as reflected in economic and sector work and analytical reports (especially from the Poverty Reduction and Economic Management sector and the Human Development sector). Consideration of gender issues in the labor markets has become increasingly mainstreamed (for example, "Women's Work, Education, and Family Welfare in Peru," 1991; "El Salvador–Moving to a Gender Approach: Issues and Recommendations," 1996).[6] Some of the poverty assessments and studies completed during the 1990s for countries in LAC concentrated on the link between poverty and wages— for example, "The Brazilian Labor Market in the 1980s," 1993; and "Bolivia–Poverty, Equity and Income: Selected Policies for Expanding Earning Opportunities for the Poor," 1996. Although worker-training programs are scarce or nonexistent in most countries of the region because of government fiscal constraints and lack of incentives for private sector firms, in a few countries they are quite extensive and have been the subject of analysis (for example, Trinidad and Tobago and Mexico).

The most significant area of unfunded fiscal liabilities in LAC has been the social security system. Relaxed enforcement of contribution payments and mismanagement of reserves compounded the basic imbalance between contributions and benefit payouts. The fiscal unsustainability of this situation encouraged extensive reforms in the region—it has been the most aggressive reformer, next to the ECA region—starting with Chile in 1981, which replaced its public pay-as-you-go scheme with a system of privately managed, fully funded individual accounts. More than one-third of the 23 reforms were multipillar in nature. All of the following countries, in addition to Chile, adopted some type of multipillar reform: Argentina, Bolivia, Colombia, El Salvador, Mexico, Peru, Uruguay, and Venezuela. Reforms in Ecuador, Nicaragua, and Guatemala should occur this fiscal year, and Brazil may undertake some reforms, although they are likely to be parametric rather than multipillar.

The World Bank has supported these efforts through lending, analytical, and advisory services. It has made 27 loans involving pension reform to countries of the region

(Argentina, Bolivia, Brazil, Colombia, Costa Rica, El Salvador, Honduras, Mexico, Panama, Peru, and Uruguay); it has produced at least 16 economic and sector work reports and some 23 regional or country-specific papers covering diverse aspects of pension reform. In many countries, second-generation reforms are now on the agenda to address issues such as low coverage—on average, the systems cover only 38 percent of the economically active population and provide pensions to about 31 percent of the population over age 60—and problems caused by regulations on pension fund managers that have produced segmented financial markets, high commercialization costs, and insufficient choice for the beneficiaries.

The LAC region has a long history of providing safety nets to the poor. The World Bank has conducted analysis of social assistance in country economic and sector work, poverty assessments, and special regional studies.[7] In fact, as a general rule, when there is a poverty assessment for a given country, it is more likely that the country assistance strategy will have a significant poverty orientation. Assessments that contain a detailed poverty profile and relevant policy analysis have the greatest influence on lending.[8] Employment schemes or public works programs and in-kind benefit transfers have received considerable World Bank support in the region, and they have been the subject of comprehensive study and cross-country evaluation.[9] The social investment fund approach originated in the region in Bolivia in 1986, and most LAC countries adopted it over time. Some countries are already in the fourth generation of World Bank-funded social funds projects, making this region the clear leader in terms of the application of this instrument. Not surprisingly, much of the evaluatory work on social investment funds has concentrated on LAC, given its depth and range of experiences.[10]

MIDDLE EAST AND NORTH AFRICA

During the oil boom, high economic growth rates and oil revenues allowed governments in the Middle East and North Africa region countries to establish a wide array of social protection mechanisms. In labor markets, governments often used public employment as a means of supporting social welfare—for example, public sector employment was as high as 59 percent in Algeria and 47 percent in Jordan in 1995. Almost universally, they also created large vocational education and training programs. The main program and policy interventions in terms of safety nets have involved public works, microcredit and microenterprise, general food subsidies (although some countries have reduced them substantially in recent years, such as Yemen, or replaced them with targeted safety net schemes, such as Jordan and Algeria), cash, and in-kind transfers. Pay-as-you-go public pension systems cover 20-50 percent of the labor force. Although the region still has a young demographic structure, pension reform is on the agenda due to problems presented by financial sustainability, poor design, and management. These problems include loose eligibility, weak benefit-contribution link, benefit rates that are too high, and poor returns on reserves.

Much of the World Bank's assistance to the region in the social protection sector has been in the area of labor markets, including vocational and technical education. Country economic memoranda and sector reports have frequently concentrated on the problems of declining levels of employment and household income, occasioned in part by reduced economic growth and employment generation, continued rapid population growth, and declines in worker remittances (in countries with significant migration).[11] Many projects approved during the past 10 years relate either directly to employment (for example, the Algeria Rural Employment Project) or incorporate a labor market component—the latter type of project constitutes the majority. Sector work has begun to directly handle the issue of reform of the vocational and technical education sector (for example, Iran–Education, Training and the Labor Markets), and there are several active projects in this area (for example, Jordan–Training and Employment Support Project; Lebanon–Vocational and Technical Education Project; Tunisia–Second Training and Employment Project; Republic of Yemen–Vocational Training Project; and Morocco–Private Sector Development III).

Other economic and sector work and projects relate to poverty reduction and safety net provision. The World Bank produced poverty reports for several countries over the past few years (Jordan, 1994; Morocco, 1994; Tunisia, 1995; Yemen, 1996; and Algeria, 1999), has completed poverty updates for Jordan (2000), Morocco (2000), and Tunisia (2000), and is preparing a poverty note for Lebanon (2001). It completed a regional study on Consumer Food Subsidies (1999) and a Regional Social Protection Strategy, which it will disseminate within the Region (2000/2001). In 1999, the Bank prepared a social protection strategy note for Algeria and is in the process of producing a similar note for Morocco (2000).[12]

Old-age income protection has been the subject of relatively less analysis and intervention, partly as a result of the region's young population structure. Until now, there have been two loans relating to pension reform: Morocco–Contractual Development Savings Loan Project (1998); and Tunisia–Economic and Financial Reforms Support Loan Project (1991). Recently the World Bank approved an Institutional Development Fund project for Tunisia to help launch the reform of the social security system (pension and health insurance). World Bank policy papers and sector and economic reports covering pension issues include "Egypt–Country Economic Memorandum: Issues in Sustaining Economic Growth," 1997; "Options for Pension Reform in Tunisia," 1993; and "Tunisia's Insurance Sector," 1995.

The future pipeline for lending and nonlending activities is weak because governments in the MENA region still give fairly low priority to social protection, especially for borrowing. Moreover, some sector work, originally scheduled for FY01, has been delayed because of recent budgetary cuts (Tunisia–labor market and unemployment study; Iran–social safety net study). Future work should involve a pension study for West Bank and Gaza (FY01). Upcoming lending activities include Morocco–Social Fund Project (FY01) and Djibouti–Pension Reform, as a component of the Structural Adjustment Credit (FY02).

SOUTH ASIA

The fundamental development challenge facing the South Asia region is alleviating deep and widespread poverty, in part through the application of instruments of social risk management. Around 70-75 percent of the total population lives in rural areas, and many, being poor, are vulnerable to even marginal income fluctuations. Vulnerability and poverty combine to foster insecurity. A domestic calamity (such as a breadwinner's illness or death) or a community-wide scourge (drought, flood, or crop failure, for instance) can quickly erase the hard-won gains of individuals striving to overcome poverty.

A very strong correlate of poverty and vulnerability in the region is the fact that a large majority of the workers are in the informal sector, where they find mainly subsistence employment and are exposed to high risks of unemployment. The risks of unemployment and underemployment and their linkage to poverty have made the labor market a primary concern for government. Adding to the attention received by the labor market are the issues of core labor standards and child labor.

In this context, it is not surprising that much of the World Bank's analytical and advisory work in the region has historically concentrated on the labor market. Some early reports included: "Bangladesh–Raising the Level of Output and Employment in Small Scale Industry," 1973; "Poverty and Unemployment in India: An Analysis of Recent Evidence," 1980; "Public Policy and the Evolution of the Labour Market in Sri Lanka," 1986; "Small Farmers and the Landless in South Asia," 1979; and "The Evolution of Labor Markets in India," 1981. More recent reports have looked at labor market policies for higher employment in Bangladesh, labor retrenchment among state-owned enterprises and unemployment in Sri Lanka, returns to human capital in Pakistan's rural wage labor market, and poverty reduction and gender differences in the labor market in India. The World Bank's (relatively small) social protection portfolio in the region has also emphasized projects with employment generation components, often in rural areas.

Government safety net programs designed to mitigate and cope with the risks of unemployment and other broader categories of risk have involved public works, subsidies, and, to a limited extent, direct transfer programs. Public works programs have met with reasonable success while credit subsidies, food transfer and price support programs have encountered more difficulties due to their sometimes distortionary nature and benefits leakage. Public works programs like Maharashtra's Employment Guarantee Scheme in India, which have met with considerable success, have been analyzed in some detail by a number of Bank studies. The World Bank has long held an interest in short-term employment projects in the region ("Rural Works Program in South Asia," 1978, and "Reaching the Rural Poor through Public Employment: Arguments, Evidence and Lessons from South Asia," 1991) and has examined the use of labor-intensive means of road construction. It has studied India's public distribution system and the ability of its social service system to reach the poor.

Financial intermediation has also been popular, and the region has pioneered positive experiences in the area of microcredit. A World Bank study[13] reports that, as of 1997, there were 98 microfinance institutions that had US$900 million in 2.8 million outstanding loans, out of which the Grameen Bank in Bangladesh alone provided 74 percent of all loans to its 2.1 million clients. Credit programs and rural poverty, especially in Bangladesh and India, have been an important area of research by the World Bank. By providing credit, successful experiments

in microfinance link participants with market institutions and enable them to make optimum use of resources. Recently, there has also been a move toward extending the scope of microfinance beyond credit, and into providing saving and insurance services among the vulnerable poor, using similar group-based mechanisms devised at the community level. Some experiments on this front are occurring in South Asia, and researchers both within and outside the Bank have started analyzing the potential of such efforts.

Formal safety nets like public pension schemes in the region reach only a small portion of the population and represent a comparatively less pressing priority in the face of other social protection issues. Governments have solicited little assistance from the World Bank in terms of pension reform. This will likely appear on the agenda soon, however, probably first in countries such as India and Sri Lanka.

Upcoming work on vulnerability in the region will include an empirical analysis, based on panel data from Pakistan, which will attempt to measure vulnerability and track its indicators. Developing a satisfactory measure of vulnerability along with its indicators will help in designing interventions that explicitly address the issue of risk, with the objective of mitigating and coping with risk. This work will be a part of the broader agenda of the Poverty Assessment of Pakistan that the South Asia Region staff of the World Bank plans to complete by the end of the year 2001.

SUB-SAHARAN AFRICA

As in South Asia, the social protection issues in the Sub-Saharan Africa region relate fundamentally to entrenched poverty and vulnerability to natural shocks, such as drought and famine. Moreover, the region has contended with slow economic growth, macroeconomic shocks, war and civil conflict, epidemic disease (mainly AIDS), and extensive child labor. Given the limited public budgets and scope for transfer-based safety nets and the young populations of African countries, social assistance and pension programs have not been as significant as labor market programs.

World Bank attention to labor market issues has encompassed a range of topics. Several recent regional reports have looked at pay and employment reform (privatization and retrenchment) in the public sector. Other topics have included labor-based methods for roads works, aspects of employment (Ghana, Côte d'Ivoire, Malawi), child labor (Ghana, Côte d'Ivoire) and training

(Zimbabwe). The World Bank has also financed projects in public works and employment (Burkina Faso, Gambia, Mali, Niger, Senegal) and training (Madagascar, Kenya).

Analytical and advisory activities relating to social safety nets have emphasized community consultations and institutional analysis of local nongovernmental organizations (for example, Ethiopia and Nigeria). The World Bank has financed operations in social action or post-conflict recovery in several countries (including Angola, Burundi, Chad, Djibouti, Ethiopia, Madagascar, Malawi, and Zambia) and food security projects in others (Madagascar and Rwanda).

The region has the youngest population profile in the world, and pension systems reach only a small segment of the labor market, mainly the public formal sector. Although structuring and reforming pension systems has not been a priority, the issue of old-age care is assuming greater importance, especially considering the phenomenon of skip-generation households formed when income earners die due to AIDS. Children and adolescents can provide certain types of assistance to the elderly but are unable to fill the gap in terms of income generation.

NOTES FROM ANNEX TWO

[1] World Bank (1998): *East Asia: The Road to Recovery; World Bank* (2000): East Asia: Recovery and Beyond.

[2] The countries of the region fall into two main groups, European and Eurasian, which differ in terms of initial conditions at the start of transition and the path of reform followed during the 1990s. For example, the European countries generally had better institutional and administrative capacity, experienced lower declines in GDP, and undertook more aggressive reform in areas of social protection. Still, both groups face the basic common problems posed by the transition, and this section does not develop sharp distinctions between the two groups.

[3] Barr, N., ed. (1994): *Labor Markets and Social Policy in Central and Eastern Europe: The Transition and Beyond*, New York: Oxford University Press.

[4] See, for example, Allison, C. and D. Ringold (1996): *Labor Markets in Transition in Central and Eastern Europe: 1989-1995*, World Bank Technical Paper No. WTP 352, *Social Challenges of Transition Series*, World Bank, Washington, D.C.; Rutkowski, J. J. (1995): *Changes in the Wage Structure During Economic Transition in Central and Eastern Europe*, World Bank Technical Paper No. WTP 340, Social Challenges of Transition Series, World Bank, Washington, D.C.

[5] An example of a comprehensive look at the field is: Guasch, J. (1999): *Labor Market Reform and Job Creation: The Unfinished Agenda in Latin America and Caribbean Countries*, The World Bank, Finance, Private Sector, and Infrastructure, Washington, D.C.

[6] Also, see Psacharopolous, G. and C. Winter (1992): "Women's Employment and Pay in Latin America," *Finance and Development, A Quarterly Publication of the International Monetary Fund and the World Bank*, 29.

[7] For example: Grosh, M. (1994): *Administering Targeted Social Programs in Latin America: From Platitudes to Practice, Regional and Sectoral Studies*, The World Bank; Subbarao, K. and others (1997): *Safety Net Programs and Poverty Reduction: Lessons from Cross-Country Experience*, The World Bank; Baker, J. (1997): "Poverty Reduction and Human Development in the Caribbean: A Cross-Country Study," World Bank Discussion Paper No. WDP 366; de Ferranti, D., G.E. Perry, I.S. Gill, and L. Servén (2000): *Securing Our Future in a Global Economy*, The World Bank.

[8] Dayton, J,. A. Khan, H. Ribe, M. Schneider (1993): "Country Policies for Poverty Reduction—A Review of Poverty Assessments, Education, and Social Policy," Department Discussion Paper Series No. 15, The World Bank.

[9] Baker, J. (2000): *Evaluating the Poverty Impact of Projects: A Handbook for Practitioners*, The World Bank.

[10] See, for example: Glaessner, P., et al. (1994): "Poverty Alleviation and Social Investment Funds: The Latin American Experience." World Bank Discussion Paper No. 261; Subbarao *op cit.* chapter 6; Rawlings, L., L. Sherburne-Benz, and J. Van Domelen (2000): "Evaluating Social Fund Performance Across Countries: Recent Findings and Impact Evaluation Results." World Bank draft report. Processed.

[11] Examples include: "Morocco—Country Economic Memorandum: Towards Higher Growth and Employment," (1995); "Growing Faster, Finding Jobs: Choices for Morocco," (publication, 1996); "Egypt—Country Economic Memorandum: Issues in Sustaining Economic Growth," (1997); "Jordan—Issues of Employment and Labor Market Imbalances," (1986); "Jordan—Efficiency and Equity of Government Revenues and Social Expenditures," (1986).

[12] The World Bank finances social investment funds in several countries (Algeria, Egypt, West Bank and Gaza, and Yemen). Program priorities differ depending on country circumstances. Also, Yemen has an IDA-financed public works program, and Morocco has a World Bank-financed social priority project that supports public works. In addition, an IDA credit is supporting an innovative "child disability/youth-at-risk project" in Egypt.

[13] Fidler, P., and J. Paxton (1997): "An Inventory of Microfinance Institutions in South Asia," Sustainable Banking with the Poor project, World Bank, Washington, D.C.

68

APPLICATION OF THE

SOCIAL RISK MANAGEMENT MATRIX

TO WORLD REGIONS

Through the use of the social risk management matrix (Chapter 2), this section compares the present status of social risk management arrangements and strategies in the world regions and the potential for improving them. The regions are grouped in some cases to facilitate comparison.

EUROPE AND CENTRAL ASIA AND EAST ASIA AND THE PACIFIC

Countries in the ECA and EAP regions broadly share a similar income level but have very different social risk management provisions.

During the era of central planning, social risk management in ECA countries consisted mainly of risk prevention through public institutions (public ownership of the means of production, quantity planning, price setting, trade monopoly, and an absence of financial markets). There was some risk mitigation through a comprehensive set of social security programs but little risk coping (essentially for narrowly defined deserving groups). This attempted isolation from economic risk had its price in terms of economic and social development. Moreover, the transition in the former Soviet Union countries toward market-oriented economies has revealed the social consequences of the absence of the broader set of social risk management instruments. While there has already been a move away from excessive risk prevention, there is still a need to adjust the now dysfunctional social security programs and enhance the public risk-coping programs (such as social assistance) in many countries. Equally important, governments should develop market-oriented instruments, of which there is a present deficiency, and strengthen informal mechanisms (a "leftward" move in Table 2.2). In the past, market-based instruments have had very little importance in

these countries, and governments have often consciously undermined informal mechanisms, including family structures.

This situation sharply contrasts with that of many countries in the EAP region (except the transition economies of China and Indochina, which share many features with ECA countries). Informal mechanisms, mostly in the form of extended family relations, play the most important role in risk management in EAP, supported by relatively wide access to financial assets and limited public provisions (essentially only for public sector workers and a few formal private sector workers). This suggests that EAP countries should move within the social risk management matrix toward more market-based and public provision (in other words, move away from relying largely on the left-hand column in Table 2.2). With aging populations and the gradually waning importance of traditional family support in these countries, market-based and public provisions will assume increasing importance. The lack of appropriate social safety net-type provisions became particularly noticeable during the recent financial crisis. Furthermore, EAP countries should put more emphasis on risk prevention strategies, such as disaster prevention, elimination of harmful child labor, and skill enhancement (in other words, they should make an upward move in the social risk management matrix).

SUB-SAHARAN AFRICA AND SOUTH ASIA

The AFR and SAR regions are similar in income levels and social risk management situations in the matrix. They both rely on informal social risk management for large parts of their populations, have few public programs (only for the lucky few in the public sector, which is somewhat larger in the francophone countries than in other countries), and lack sufficient resources to provide large-scale social assistance to alleviate the symptoms of poverty. The two regions also share the feature of an oftendysfunctional financial sector with heavy government involvement and a limited capacity to provide market-based instruments. This would imply that they need to concentrate their fiscal resources on alleviating deep poverty, reducing risk (for example, through measures to eliminate harmful child labor), and increasing market-based social risk management mechanisms such as safe financial assets and microfinance. Gender-based violence and constraints on women's access to productive resources are major issues in both regions.

THE MIDDLE EAST AND NORTH AFRICA

The MENA countries are characterized by relatively large welfare states and strong interfamily networks (focused in the left- and right-hand columns in Table 2.2 with relatively little in the middle, market-based column). The trend of public involvement began after the oil boom of the 1970s, when governments used high oil revenues to expand social services and public sector employment. The subsequent decline in oil revenues forced most of the countries in the region to reverse this policy, but the private sector was unable to generate the new jobs required to absorb the rapidly growing labor forces. Informal sector employment and open unemployment have been on the rise since then. Today, social risk management consists mainly of informal, extended family arrangements and publicly provided schemes, although these are less prevalent than in the past. Market-based social risk management arrangements are still developing. Issues of particular importance include pensions and insurance (both of which have important implications for the labor market, old-age security, and the financial/capital markets), labor policies, skills development, and the creation of targeted, effective, and cost-efficient social assistance programs.

LATIN AMERICA AND THE CARIBBEAN

Countries in the LAC region are very heterogeneous with regard to both their income levels and the public provision of social risk management mechanisms. Many countries implemented OECD-type public arrangements early in the development process, but the share of formal employment in the labor force is still around 50 percent on average, indicating the continued high importance of informal social risk management. This indicates the need for these countries to focus less on government-provided risk mitigation measures (and the implied contribution rates to social security programs) and informal provisions, while promoting more market-based risk mitigation and coping instruments (in other words, a move away from the left and right sides of the social risk management matrix). It would also be advantageous to these countries to strengthen social safety nets for potential crisis situations, on the one hand, and to give more attention to reducing risks, on the other (in other words, make vertical moves in the matrix).

SUMMARY OF REGIONAL STRATEGIES

Region	Context and Diagnosis (Emphasis on SP Issues)	SRM and SP Arrangements	Bank Support with SP Instruments	Implications/ Future Directions
South Asia (SAR)	The South Asia region shares some characteristics with the Africa region in terms of level of socioeconomic development. Poverty is deep and widespread in a large population base, and vulnerability is a key concept, considering the large numbers of people near the poverty line for whom even marginal income fluctuations can have serious consequences. This applies predominantly to the rural sector—it holds 70-75% of the total population, which is very susceptible to risks from natural sources (for example, flooding, crop failure, etc.). There is also considerable poverty among the urban population, which faces a different set of risks. Child labor is prevalent. The role of the state in the economy has generally been heavy-handed, which has created certain distortions. Financial markets have traditionally been weak. Public sector performance has been problematic.	**Informal** (family, community, and market-based) arrangements are common but in some circumstances may be prejudicial, for example, exploitative power structures, unequal social rights. Limited budgetary capacity has largely prohibited **government provision** of significant social-assistance type arrangements, and a dysfunctional financial sector, resulting in part from government overinvolvement, offers limited formal **market-based** instruments of social risk management. Public efforts in social risk management have focused on the **labor market** (mainly through employment generation in rural areas), subsidies, and, to a limited extent, direct transfer programs. The most prominent type of intervention has been public works programs, which have met with reasonable success in the region. **Credit subsidies and food transfer and price support programs** have met with relatively less success becaue of their sometimes distortionary nature, difficulties in targeting, and possibilities for corruption. **Financial intermediation** has also been popular, and the region has pioneered positive experiences in the area of microcredit. **Public pension schemes** reach only a small portion of the population and represent a comparatively less pressing priority in the face of other social protection issues.	The Bank's SP portfolio in South Asia is the smallest of all regions, with around 25 projects approved—either pure SP or with SP components—since 1991 (at least one in every country). Most of these are projects in the **agriculture** sector (predominantly in India) that involve **public works** components, although there are also projects from the transportation, water supply, sanitation and environment sectors. Sri Lanka and India have both had pure SP projects, in **poverty alleviation** and **rural women's development**, respectively.	**Public works** programs in rural areas will likely remain an important mechanism of social risk management. It would be sensible for other public efforts to focus on deep poverty and vulnerable groups (for example, child labor). Building on successful experiences with microcredit, financial intermediation will likely explore possibilities to introduce **safe savings** and insurance mechanisms to the poor. **Group-based insurance**, which induces peer monitoring and reduces moral hazard problems, has already begun to appear in the region. **Social investment funds** may provide a vehicle for addressing poverty alleviation. To date, South Asian countries have not adopted this instrument, which is widely used in other regions. **Formal insurance and pension arrangements** will not receive as much attention, at least in the short term. Still, existing public systems suffer typical problems and would benefit from reform.

71

Region	Context and Diagnosis (Emphasis on SP Issues)	SRM and SP Arrangements	Bank Support with SP Instruments	Implications/ Future Directions
East Asia and the Pacific (EAP)	Rapid and sustained economic growth over the past several decades was the primary means of socioeconomic improvement and social protection. Governments had little incentive to plan for downside risks and also relied on strong informal, family-based arrangements. Widespread public provision of education and health services allowed the remarkable rise in living standards. The East Asia financial crisis revealed that reliance solely on growth was not enough to ensure sustained poverty reduction, existing formal safety nets were dramatically inadequate and lack of them in some countries made the effects worse, and informal coping mechanisms have their limits. Poverty still remains at high levels in several countries including the Philippines, Vietnam, Cambodia, Lao PDR, and Mongolia. In high-growth countries, vulnerability to poverty remains high given the large numbers of households just above the poverty line and rising inequality. Vulnerable groups have emerged or increased in significance (e.g., youth, migrants, refugees, working and urban poor). Industrial relations systems and core labor standard enforcement are weak, contributing, for example, to the continued existence of child labor and high worker injury rates. Aging (the old-age dependency ratio for EAP trails only that of ECA), urbanization and formalization of labor may weaken informal risk management mechanisms. Three groups of economies have somewhat different characteristics, SP arrangements, and corresponding needs: **emerging market economies** (the East Asia Crisis 5— Indonesia, Republic of Korea, Malaysia, the Philippines, and Thailand); **transition economies** (Cambodia, China, Lao PDR, Mongolia, and Vietnam); and **small market economies** (Papua New Guinea and the Pacific Islands). (The Bank does not work with the high-income countries, or the Democratic People's Republic of Korea or Myanmar.)	**Labor market policies** in the emerging market economies have achieved good relative flexibility, and education and training have largely met demand. Growth in labor productivity has been shared with workers. The small Pacific economies are comparatively very rigid, and regulations still impede mobility and wage flexibility in transition economies despite reform. To varying degrees, governments have begun to take on the problems of child labor, enforcement of core labor standards, and encouragement of a stronger labor relations framework. The emerging market economies have utilized job search assistance, public works schemes, and small enterprise development programs. Some countries have recently experimented with unemployment insurance. **Public pension systems** fall into the following categories: National Provident Fund systems (Indonesia, Malaysia, Papua New Guinea); social security-type systems in evolution (Korea, Philippines, and Thailand); and social security-type systems in transition economies (China, Lao PDR, Cambodia, Mongolia, and Vietnam). The provident funds provide very low levels of benefits. Weak benefit-contribution links characterize the SS Systems in Evolution, leading to fiscal problems. In the transition economies, systems are largely unfunded and have represented large burdens for the state-owned enterprises. Other problems common to most systems include: poor design; separate and generous civil service pensions; lack of annuities; poor investment of reserves; generally low coverage. A variety of formal **safety net programs** (i.e., public works, food security, cash transfers and social funds) exist in the emerging market economies, although they are limited in scale and coverage. The transition economies have largely relied on state-owned enterprises and collective agriculture to satisfy social welfare needs. Strong **informal, community-based support systems** (e.g., wantok and matai) have been the mainstay of the small market economies in terms of social risk management.	Before the crisis, the Bank's social protection portfolio in the region emphasized labor markets above other areas, mainly as a function of country preferences, and many projects involved **labor market** components. Crisis-related adjustment lending has concentrated on SP, which represented over 80% of the US$11 billion lent since 12/97. Loans to Korea took an integrated approach with pension reform, unemployment and health insurance, and safety net components. Support for **pension reform** has been limited (involving only three operations), although economic and sector work has taken on the issue in China, Mongolia, and the Philippines. The adjustment loans have addressed **safety net** concerns, including a US$600 million loan to Indonesia solely for safety net reform. Several investment operations in other countries preceded the crisis. Interest in **social investment funds** is increasing, with projects in Cambodia, Indonesia, Lao PDR, the Philippines, and Thailand. Despite these trends, poverty assessments for the EAP countries are generally outdated—an exception is Thailand, where the 1996 poverty assessment used empirical data to evaluate anti-poverty programs and suggested their reorientation to achieve better results. Currently, Bank staff are preparing poverty updates for Cambodia, Indonesia, Lao PDR, and Papua New Guinea.	**Labor market issues** will continue to be of special interest to both the emerging market and transition economies, respectively, because of the continuous need to protect vulnerable people, which the crisis intensified, and the problems posed by redundant labor in the transition. Special topics such as child labor, core labor standards, and labor relations will continue to demand attention. Some of the emerging market economies—Korea, the Philippines, and Thailand—are becoming more concerned with the financial sustainability of their PAYG **social security systems,** and the same holds true for China, Mongolia, and Vietnam, in which state-owned enterprises have encountered difficulties meeting their obligations during the transition. The reform agenda for pensions is large and includes the strengthening of institutional capability and moves toward more sustainable multipillar options. **Social safety** nets have assumed greater significance after the crisis in the emerging market economies and will remain important in the transition economies in the context of increased dismantling of enterprise-based social assistance, as in China and Vietnam. Social funds are catching on in both emerging market and transition countries. So far the **small market economies** have done very little in the way of developing formal social protection interventions, but they will face the typical challenges in the future and must currently deal with special problems such as youth unemployment.

72

Region	Context and Diagnosis (Emphasis on SP Issues)	SRM and SP Arrangements	Bank Support with SP Instruments	Implications/ Future Directions
Africa (AFR)	**Broad development challenges:** ■ Poverty ■ Slow economic growth, on the periphery of global economy ■ Macroeconomic shocks ■ War and civil conflict ■ Highest population growth rate of regions ■ Young population, small portion of elderly, decline of reproductive age population due to AIDS ■ Epidemic disease: AIDS (esp. southern and eastern regions), resulting in loss of incomeearners, production of orphans and "skip-generation" households; malaria (esp. in western region) ■ Drought, famine, and seasonal shortages ■ Idiosyncratic risk in context of inequitable informal risk management arrangements (for example, death of husband when inheritance laws are unfair to women) ■ Child labor	**Informal arrangements** (diversified income strategies; savings in either highly liquid or nonliquid forms; coping through draw-down of physical and human capital; risk-averse production choices; mutual or co-insurance with friends or relatives; higher fertility to provide labor and possibility of intergenerational transfer; borrowing and gift exchange) For the poor these arrangements are often costly, relatively ineffective, inequitable, self-limiting, and may harm long-term human capital formation, bear negative externalities (i.e. problem of abuse of the commons), and fail when most needed. **Formal arrangements:** ■ Limited scope for transfer-based safety nets nationally given low average incomes, large proportions of population in poverty and small size of wealthy class (except to some degree in middle-income countries, e.g., South Africa, Namibia, Botswana, Swaziland) ■ Price controls and subsidies on consumer goods and agricultural production have not been well targeted, and free food programs have developed dependency and modified production behavior ■ Minimum wage and job security regulations have benefited a small group of privileged formal sector workers while reducing employment growth ■ Public works programs have not been widely used and, when used, design flaws have limited effectiveness ■ Subsidized microcredit programs have been emphasized at the expense of microsavings; meanwhile, they have encountered high transaction costs due to low density and poor infrastructure, thereby not effectively reaching the poor ■ Small-scale insurance schemes cover only low-cost, high-frequency events due to the inability to form a large risk pool, and they charge regressive flat premiums ■ Public and private sector pension schemes operate in most countries but reach only extremely small portions of the population and are largely fiscally unsustainable	■ SIFs and Agence d'Exécution de Travaux d'Intérêt Publique (AGETIPS), operational in about 15 countries, have created employment and improved riskreduction through the efficient provision of small-scale social and economic infrastructure but have not reached the most vulnerable groups or achieved much success in microcredit activities ■ Projects with labor market components have generated limited and mostly short-term employment ■ Social insurance and pension reform operations have been extremely limited ■ Operations in other sectors have contributed to risk reduction (for example, roads to markets) ■ There have been a few innovative operations in the area of post-conflict intervention ■ The World Bank has conducted poverty assessments in most countries, providing a basis on which to plan social policy	All of the following items represent potential growth areas for SP: ■ Systematic risk analysis at the country level to better take account of and understand household risk management behavior ■ Empirical analysis of the scale of public resources spent on formal safety nets and the number and socioeconomic profile of beneficiaries to allow reorientation of programs toward the poor ■ Planning of new operations in the area of AIDS prevention and mitigation, and adjusting existing projects, such as social funds to incorporate actions in this field (e.g., prime-age death as a targeting criterion) ■ Conflict prevention and post-conflict intervention, especially with children ■ Experimentation with new tools such as earmarked, prepaid, multirisk social protection funds ■ Testing of new forms of insurance, for example, savings accounts with withdrawal regulations associated with catastrophic or major expenditure needs ■ Structuring supply-side measures to protect basic social spending and demand-side measures to maintain consumption of services (e.g., fee waivers) after a shock ■ Assisting in the reform of civil codes and their enforcement in order to improve protection for women and children ■ Exploration of methods to prevent harmful child labor, such as the combat of child trafficking, establishment of a child labor fund, and adjustment of school calendar with agricultural cycle ■ Establishment of microsavings mechanisms ■ Enhancing drought preparedness through rural infrastructure development ■ Expanding social funds to promote positive informal insurance methods ■ Reforming existing pension systems to establish financial sustainability

73

Region	Context and Diagnosis (Emphasis on SP Issues)	SRM and SP Arrangements	Bank Support with SP Instruments	Implications/ Future Directions
Europe and Central Asia (ECA)	The dissolution of the socialist SP system and transition from planned to market economy have led to lower living standards, greater vulnerability, poverty, and unemployment. The central SP policy goal under socialism was full **labor market** employment. Subsidies to state enterprises helped achieve this objective. Since the state implicitly insured against unemployment, it did not encourage development of explicit provisions, i.e., unemployment insurance. The state determined the price of labor and job placement, which caused distortions in the labor market and skills mix. **Pension and social insurance schemes** had wide coverage but have become fiscally unsustainable in the face of loose eligibility criteria, low retirement ages, generous benefits, evasion, a weak benefit-contribution link, continued population aging, and a devastated tax base (in the case of Eurasian countries). In the context of guaranteed employment, countries did not develop market-style **safety net** structures. Rather, they used extensive subsidies on goods and services to meet basic needs, provided cash and in-kind benefits for certain vulnerable groups, and emphasized residential care for groups outside the rubric of normal life. Dismantling the subsidy system, especially in the Eastern European countries, combined with increased unemployment and poverty, neglect of residential institutions, or the significant arrears and decline in value of cash and in-kind benefits in the Eurasian countries, mean that social safety nets deserve increasing attention. State policies resulted, often purposefully, in attrition of **informal arrangements**. **European transition economies** (vs. Eurasian) have realized lower GDP declines and higher levels of income. Institutional and administrative capacity is stronger. In leading reformers, growth has resumed, and unemployment is declining. **Eurasian transition economies** have experienced falling real wages and labor productivity; growth has generally not resumed. Average income per capita is lower, and open unemployment and the informal sector are growing.	**European transition economies** have undertaken more aggressive restructuring and layoffs coupled with higher levels of SP spending in response to output declines. Strong labor market institutions, i.e., unions, collective bargaining institutions, and minimum wages, stemmed real wage declines. The creation of unemployment insurance without coordination with social assistance measures has generated incentive problems. Governments are reforming pension systems both through parametric changes and the introduction and preparation of multipillar systems. Means-tested social assistance has become the main poverty alleviation mechanism. **Eurasian transition economies** have done relatively less restructuring. Although open unemployment is lower, many workers remain with unpaid leaves and large wage arrears. Labor market institutions are weak and have been unable to stem the decline in wages. The informal economy is larger (as a share of GDP). Lack of evaluation of new widespread active labor market programs means that their effectiveness remains unknown. Pension spending still remains high relative to output, but effective protection is insignificant in real terms, with benefit payments in arrears. An exception is Kazakhstan, which switched to a privately managed, fully funded system. The safety net provides uncoordinated and overlapping benefits and services and still focuses more heavily on subsidies for housing and utilities (rather than means-tested transfers). These are not funded but are poorly administered and targeted.	Prior to the 1990s most ECA countries were not Bank clients. Bank SP work was sporadic and related mainly to labor markets and social expenditures. This changed dramatically with the dissolution of the Soviet Union and the economic transition, which resulted in the restructuring of SP systems and institutions. The Bank has funded **labor market** programs involving pre-and post layoff assistance to workers through job counseling and referral, public works, wage subsidies, small business creation, and retraining. It has helped develop systems to register unemployment, financed civil works and equipment for employment bureau, trained personnel in labor market programs, supported capacity to contract out active labor market programs, developed business incubators, and supported public works programs. Policy- based adjustment lending has focused on improving the fiscal solvency of unemployment and social insurance systems through the reduction of payroll taxes or improvement in contributions. The Bank has helped in the creation and restructuring of severance payments, respectively, in countries where enterprise was limited and where these were constraining the termination of workers. Another area of emphasis has been reform of labor relations legislation. In the area of **pension reform**, the Bank has provided technical assistance and financed reform efforts in 18 countries through stand-alone projects or adjustment loans with pension components. The Bank has been relatively less involved in work on **safety nets**, but it has provided comprehensive sector work and investment and adjustment lending in the Balkans, Romania, Russia, Kyrgyz Republic, and Kazakhstan. It has investment projects in Latvia, Lithuania, Armenia, and Georgia. There are **social investment funds** in Armenia, Georgia, Romania, Bulgaria, Moldova, Albania, and Tajikistan.	In **European transition economies**, labor market policies should focus on improving flexibility, in part through decentralization of collective bargaining and legislative reforms to reduce termination/hiring constraints. Minimum wages should be kept low. In countries that have realized growth, active labor market programs, with built-in evaluation mechanisms, should be maintained to reduce the long duration of unemployment. Pension and unemployment insurance systems should be reformed to improve their affordability and consumption- smoothing function, with benefits linked to contributions. The introduction of multipillar pension schemes will improve savings for old age and deepen capital markets. Minimum pensions and means-tested social assistance systems can be used to address poverty. However, programs should incorporate work incentives and should be fiscally affordable. De-institutionalization and the development of community based services should also be a focus of social policy. In **Eurasian transition economies**, macrostability and restructuring must precede fundamental labor market reforms. In the meantime, severance pay to spur restructuring and reforms of the labor legislation to lay the ground work for competitive market structure can be initiated. Limited tax collection and large informal economies mean that risk mitigation or consumption-smoothing programs, e.g., unemployment insurance and multipillar pensions that link contribution to benefits, are difficult to implement and sustain. Instead, social protection programs should focus on poverty relief. Flat benefits for pensions and unemployment should be considered, with unemployment benefits coordinated with severance pay. The safety net should focus on simple indicator targeting, such as child allowances. A better understanding of prevailing informal safety nets should be achieved before the introduction of new systems. Active labor market programs, given large informal economies and low labor demand, are not likely to be appropriate. Social investment funds or community works programs can help in providing temporary employment.

74

Region	Context and Diagnosis (Emphasis on SP Issues)	SRM and SP Arrangements	Bank Support with SP Instruments	Implications/ Future Directions
Latin America and the Caribbean (LAC)	Countries of the region have wide differences in terms of socioeconomic development, but they generally share several characteristics that have resulted fundamentally from a narrow and exclusive economic growth pattern. The countries have sizeable (and growing) informal labor markets (57% of workers in 1995 on average, up from 52% in 1990), persistent poverty (37% of the population of the region), where most of the poor are in urban areas (58%) but the worst poverty is rural (59% of extreme poor), very unequal income distribution (Gini in the range of 0.4 to 0.6, and on average the highest for any region in the world), and very unequal access to physical, human, and financial capital (the 7 countries with the highest concentration of land in the world are in LAC). Unemployment and underemployment have been significant in many countries, and governments have often used public employment as a relief mechanism (and as a reward for political loyalty). In addition to natural disasters, several countries have felt the shocks of recent financial and monetary crises, for example, balance of payments and exchange rate and volatility in foreign investment and private capital flows. As a result of economic crises, new groups of poor and vulnerable people are emerging.	Countries of the LAC region face a number of common challenges in social protection and have normally established a full range of programs to handle them. These have experienced largely the same difficulties, leading to similar reform efforts. ■ Many countries have been attempting to ease regulation in the formal sector **labor market**, which has historically driven growth in the informal sector, but in general progress has been modest. Reforms involve reducing taxation on labor use; enhancing flexibility in contracting, deploying and terminating workers; producing means for the peaceful resolution of labor disputes, including collective bargaining; improving severance pay systems; and addressing redundancies and quality and efficiency issues in public sector employment (partly through downsizing and training). Active labor market programs, mainly in the form of technical and vocational education and training, have been prominent in some countries but not others. ■ Fiscal unsustainability and weak benefit-contribution linkages in **public pension schemes** have contributed to widespread experimentation with reform, of which much has been under the multipillar model. Prominent "second-generation" reform issues include persistent low coverage despite shifts to full funding, high administrative costs (often associated with marketing) of pension fund management bodies, and inequity from the continued existence of special arrangements for public sector workers in many countries. ■ Governments in the region have employed all forms of **safety nets**, especially social assistance (mainly in-kind transfers) and public works, with different degrees of success regarding both coverage and targeting of the poor. Many have removed some badly targeted subsidies (e.g., food, energy) but not others (housing). The region was the first to implement the social investment fund (SIF) model both as a response to the period of structural adjustment and then as an efficient means to finance social and economic infrastructure. The SIFs built upon or complemented previously existing safety net programs. They now exist in many countries of the region.	The social protection portfolio in the LAC region is the Bank's largest, and it has projects in all the traditional areas of SP. The Bank financed technical and vocational training programs for years in the past. Many projects have included components involving the labor markets, for example, through employment creation. More recently, and as part of structural reform programs, the Bank has supported some governments' efforts to ease the **labor markets reform** process. With regard to the region's extensive efforts in **pension reform**, the Bank has made 27 loans to various countries (Argentina, Bolivia, Brazil, Colombia, Costa Rica, El Salvador, Honduras, Mexico, Panama, Peru, and Uruguay), it has produced at least 16 economic and sector work reports, and some 23 regional or country-specific papers covering diverse aspects of the subject. **Safety net programs** The Bank has encouraged and backed the implementation of the social investment fund approach in the region, and has funded SIFs in over 12 countries. In some countries it is already financing the third or fourth generation of SIF projects. In addition, protection of core social assistance expenditures, public works/employment generation, and transfer schemes are receiving increasing Bank support, largely as part of its crises response packages.	LAC countries, with a few exceptions, will need to continue their efforts to liberalize **labor markets**. The creation of insurance mechanisms for informal sector workers and severance pay arrangements for formal sector workers will remain the main priorities in terms of social risk management both in the short and medium term. Countries will progress in the first generation of **pension reform,** and some will begin to act on second generation issues, such as high administrative costs, continued low coverage due to a large informal sector labor market and unwillingness of certain groups to adhere, better annuity provision, and integration of separate public sector and civil servant schemes into the main public system. Strengthening of the financial sector will play a major role for progress in the pensions area. Governments are increasingly realizing that **social safety nets** must be in place to help them deal with the impact of crises on the poor/vulnerable, and assist those unable to help themselves. To this end, they will need to rationalize and streamline existing programs and improve budgetary allocation practices and processes, so that their funding becomes "countercyclical." Determining the future directions and role of Social Investment Funds will be a key issue. Applying adequate and transparent targeting mechanisms and reaching vulnerable groups (for example, indigenous populations) will continue to challenge safety net programs and SIFs. Other social protection issues that will require attention include child labor, increased crime and violence, and disaster prevention.

Region	Context and Diagnosis (Emphasis on SP Issues)	SRM and SP Arrangements	Bank Support with SP Instruments	Implications/ Future Directions
Middle East and North Africa (MENA)	Oil markets have exercised a large effect on the level and variability of country incomes, and determined socioeconomic trends as well as movements in labor markets. Until the mid-1980s, the MENA region benefited from high growth rates largely based on oil price increases. As a result of the oil revenues governments increased investment in the social sectors and established a whole range of formal social protection mechanisms; poverty remained lower than in other regions; the state increased its role in wage setting and created most of the employment; and population growth and high costs of providing scarce water resources was not a concern. The collapse of oil prices in the mid-1980s depressed incomes and led to low investment rates, slow—even negative—GDP growth, and increased vulnerability, poverty, and unemployment. Catastrophic shocks have also been increasing (for example, war in Iran and Iraq and conflicts in Yemen, Lebanon, and Algeria). In addition to its direct costs, conflict has also led to a reduction in out-migration (for example, Egypt and Jordan) and substantial repatriations. The economic decline has created the following questions: (a) How can productivity increase, unemployment decline, and labor incomes increase? (b) What mix of formal and informal social protection mechanisms can protect the welfare of the poor and decrease the vulnerability of both the poor and the fragile middle class? (c) What policies can restore a sustainable growth path in the region, and how can the results of growth be equitably distributed among the population?	Macroeconomic and trade policies implemented during the oil boom (i.e., expansion of public sector as a substitute for "social protection" and small private sector) have shaped labor market structure and dynamics. The rigid institutional structures have led to a rather inflexible response to labor market pressures: in the formal sector, employment growth did not match labor supply growth, while the response of real wages was slow as the labor market imbalances grew. Informal employment expanded, and poverty incidence in most countries rose. Almost universally, countries are employing large vocational education and training programs, which are expensive and out of tune with labor conditions. **Public pension systems** are based on partial funding and operate on a defined benefit, PAYG basis. They have weak links to contributions, and fund reserves are often inefficiently managed. Other problems include: poor design, generous civil servant pensions, poor investment of reserves, and low coverage. The system also creates labor market distortions due to large implicit taxation on labor, and provides incentives to move to the informal sector. **Formal safety net programs** (i.e., public works, microfinance, food subsidies, cash transfers, and social funds) have been used to provide income-earning opportunities for the unemployed, to reduce poverty, and to mitigate shocks and their effects on the most vulnerable groups. But efficiency of these programs—especially those involving subsidies—can be improved. Kinship-based networks characterize social organization in the MENA region. Households activate these networks to offset the effects of crises. These networks are of vital importance in terms of spreading and diversifying the risks, insuring against them (i.e., localized catastrophes), and strengthening, over the long term, the economic and social capital within a group that can be accessed in times of shock or stress.	■ Many Bank projects in the region relate directly to **employment** (for example, Algeria - Rural Employment Project) or have labor market components. ■ **Vocational training** has been an area of emphasis for Bank operations (Algeria, Egypt, Jordan, Lebanon, Morocco, Tunisia, and Yemen). ■ **Pension reforms** have been limited in the region, though there is increasing awareness of the need for reform (Egypt, Morocco and Tunisia). ■ **Social Investment Funds** (Algeria, Egypt, West Bank and Gaza, Yemen) have been used to mitigate shocks and their effects on the most vulnerable groups and also as compensatory mechanisms to increase access to, and the quality of, basic social and infrastructure services used by the poor. However, their operations remain small compared to the magnitude of poverty in MENA. ■ A few adjustment loans have addressed **safety net** concerns, but the efficiency of the systems still needs to be improved. ■ The Bank has conducted **poverty assessments** in most countries. However, they are generally outdated and data reliability limits their usefulness.	A key issue involves improving effectiveness of relatively large public social spending through better management of service provision and increased synergy among governments, private mechanisms, and civil society. **Labor market policies** need to facilitate efficient employment creation. To achieve this goal, employment in public enterprises needs to be rationalized and firms' adjustment costs must be reduced; nonwage labor costs need to be better aligned with desirable objectives (for example, labor market insurance) to achieve better outcomes at reduced labor costs; effective labor market programs should be used to cushion the costs of adjustment to workers (such as public works, retraining, employment services, job search assistance, self-employment support, etc). Vocational training reform is a priority, considering the associated fiscal burden and the limited links to labor demand. Improving the financial sustainability and increasing the low coverage of the PAYG **pension systems** would require the rationalization and revamping of the benefit formula, the integration of schemes or the harmonization of benefits across schemes, and a move toward multipillar systems. **Social safety nets** need to be better monitored and evaluated. Microfinance should be part of a country's financial sector development strategy; public works need to use self-targeting mechanisms more efficiently to attract the poor; sustainability of social funds needs to be improved; food subsidies need to be linked to a broad poverty alleviation strategy; and the coverage of social assistance needs to be increased.

76

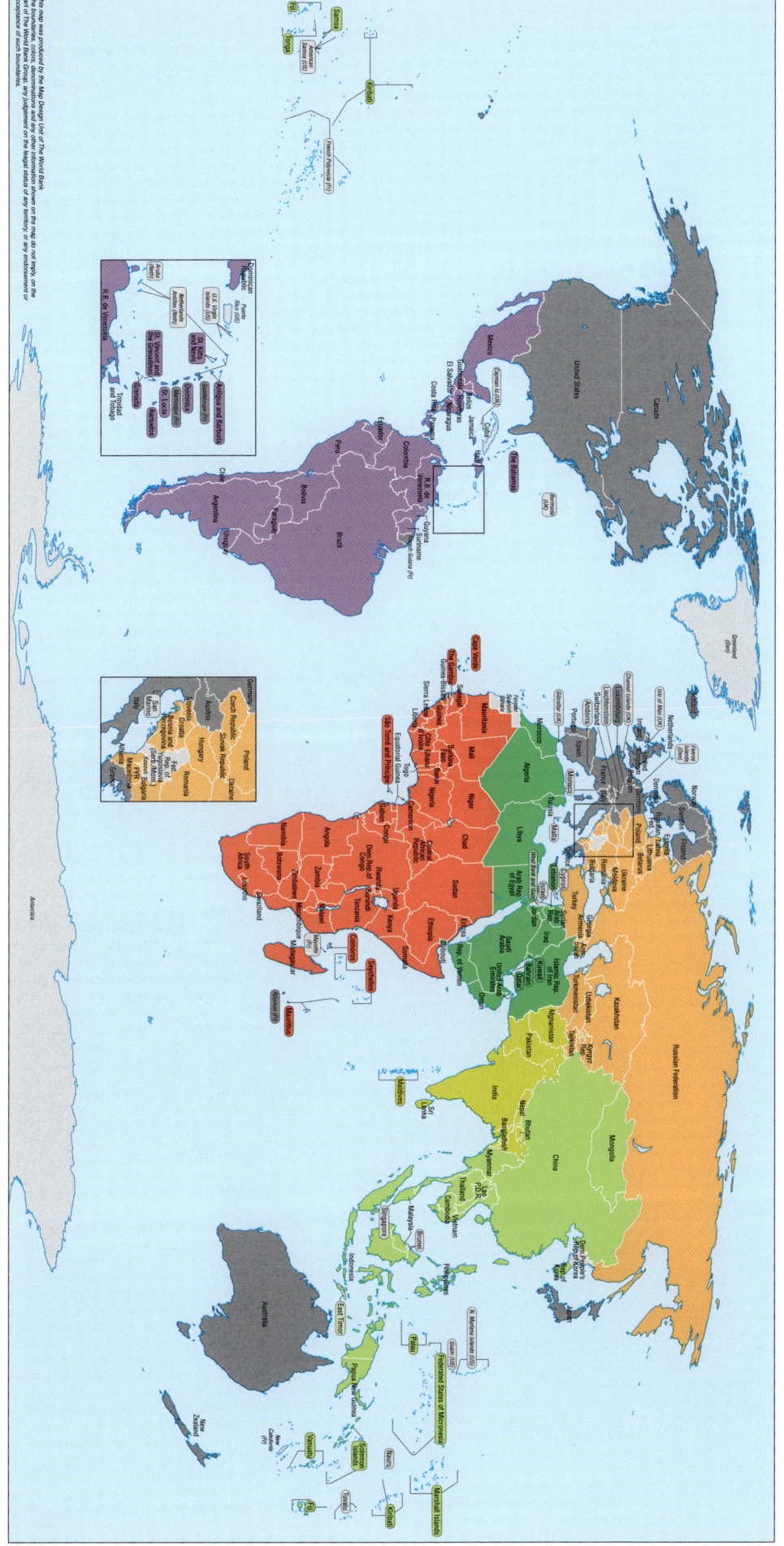

World Bank Regions

- Latin America and the Caribbean Region
- Europe and Central Asia Region
- Middle East and North Africa Region
- Africa Region
- South Asia Region
- East Asia and Pacific Region
- OECD High-income economies
- Other